BEYOND THE GREEN HORIZON

Principles for sustainable tourism

Edited by Shirley Eber

A discussion paper commissioned from
Tourism Concern by WWF UK

EDITORIAL ADVISORY GROUP

Tricia Barnett, Janet Cochrane, Shirley Eber

Clive Gordon, Margaret Leighfield, Richard Tapper

EDITORIAL TEAM

Tricia Barnett, Kim Inglis, Margaret Leighfield

The opinions expressed in this discussion paper are those of Tourism Concern, and do not necessarily represent those of WWF or any of the consultees or contributors

The opinions expressed in each case study are those of the named author(s) and do not necessarily represent those of Tourism Concern or WWF

Acknowledgments

The work of the following contributors has been used and integrated into the text of this book. Individuals are acknowledged separately in the bibliography where specific cases are cited in the text. Tourism Concern warmly thanks all contributors to this publication:

Dr. Gerald Bonang, Atma Jaya Catholic University, Malaysia

Dr. Bill Bramwell, Sheffield Hallam University, England

Hilary Bradt, Bradt Publications, England

Professor Lino Briguglio, Malta University, Malta

Paul Cleave, Exeter College, England

Polly Davies, Marco Polo Travel Service, England

Mark Eckstein, Cobham Resource Consultants, England

John Forrest, Tambopata Reserve Society, England

Dr. Tim Forsyth, University College London, England

Syd House, The Good Tourist Guide Books, Scotland

Arwel Jones, Arwel Jones Associates, Wales

Eva Fleg Lambert, Resident, Isle of Skye, Scotland

Bernard Lane, University of Bristol, England

Judith Lim, Induk Refleksi Dan Inspirasi, Indonesia

Dr. James McCarthy, Nature Conservancy Council, Scotland

Bill Martin and Sandra Mason, Leisure Consultants, England

Dr. Roger Millman, Centre for the Advancement of Responsive Travel, England

Dr. Michael Parnwell, University of Hull, England

Anita Pleumaron, Tourism, Development and Environment Project, Bangkok

Julia Robson, Vacations for Wildlife, England

Dr. M. Thea Sinclair, University of Kent, England

Dr. Hugh Somerville, British Airways, England

Colin and Fleur Speakman, Transport for Leisure Ltd, England

Ian Thomas, Rhwyney Valley Tourist Association, Wales

Dr. John Towner, University of Northumbria at Newcastle, England

Simon Woodward, Frontline Management Consultants Ltd, Scotland

Artemis Yiordamlis and Adrian Akers-Douglas, Laona Project, Cyprus

And thanks to Rachel Leighfield who prepared this manuscript and Dr. Tom Selwyn for his advice.

We are also grateful to the following for their comments and advice: Peggy Allcott, Ishak Arifan, Janet Barber, Barry Coates, Carol Hatton, Martin Mathers, Gail Murray, Rachel Okunlola, Sian Pullen, Peter Ramshaw, Sally Richardson, Tessa Robertson, Gill Witter, Gaynor Whyles, Clive Wicks and Marguerite Young.

There are few topics so widely debated today as that of the rapid deterioration of the earth's natural resources: the global focus on this issue resulted in the largest ever gathering of politicians, scientists, ecological activists and others at Rio de Janeiro in June 1992.

Although tourism, as an issue, was not high on the agenda – either at the official UNCED meeting or the parallel Global Forum – it was reflected in statements such as the Kari-Oca Declaration and Indigenous Peoples Earth Charter which preceded the Earth Summit.

Nevertheless, the importance of tourism as an issue remains undiminished. The implication of this for people concerned about tourism – and there are many, both in sending and receiving countries – is that we must work harder, both to give it due recognition and to ensure action in response.

Clearly, this can only happen with a better understanding of what constitutes tourism as a phenomenon, as an industrial-economic activity and structure, its relevance to a world in transformation, and its impacts and consequences on destinations and people.

This discussion paper attempts to articulate some of the complexities of modern tourism, though its scope is limited to examining economic structures, and the socio-economic and environmental consequences that result from tourism as an industrial activity.

It suggests alternative policies for tourism development, as well as guidelines on how these might be implemented, drawing from the experiences of such examples as the Annapurna Conservation Area project in Nepal and the 'Tourism for Discovery' project in Senegal.

Whether these endeavours can shape the future of tourism remains to be seen. For the moment, they merely pay 'lip service to the need for more radical change', to quote the Senegal case. Practitioners of so-called 'alternative tourism' such as Chayant Pholpoke of Life Travel in Thailand, have warned that it is even more destructive than mass tourism,

since it brings tourists into direct contact with people in remote locations, thus intensifying acculturation and its attendant effects.

Pholpoke echoes critics who suggest that alternative tourism cannot satisfy the tourist's quest for authenticity, but rather serves to push the quest even further back.

Within the debate on Third World tourism, much of the cultural critique of tourism centres on the notion of a 'static' culture: one which is often romanticised as being in harmony with nature, non-exploitative, and which has remained unchanged for centuries. The existence of hierarchical structures – ethnic or class-based – has rarely been recognised when recommendations are made, for example, in relation to 'local participation' in decision-making.

Demands for reverting to 'tradition' – heard all too often within tourism debates today – might, in effect, contribute to retention of traditional structures of exploitation and control.

More than this, there is no established way of ensuring that an alternative today does not become the norm tomorrow. This is especially true in Third World nations which have little ability to influence and guide their own 'development'. Bhutan and China, once cited as shining examples of 'controlled tourism' are as keen to get tourists and multinational investments as any other nation in Asia. The collapse of the Soviet Union has seen the opening of both the Balkan and Baltic states, as well as of Central and Eastern Europe.

And as is well-known, destinations which are today the subject of some of the fiercest debates – Goa, Bali, Katmandu – were once the haunts of yesterday's world traveller.

Realistically speaking, the critique of tourism has to incorporate a much deeper understanding of socio-cultural and political processes than that which exists. Moreover, it can ill afford to ignore the fact that tourism is growing, and has grown even more in places which have been publicised by the debate – such as Goa.

To my mind, the concern for tourism must now shift into areas not touched so far by the debate: areas which perhaps lie outside the apparent sphere of tourism. Be that as it may, it is essential that the tourism industry addresses the problems within its domain.

Paul Gonsalves, Coordinator, EQUATIONS
Bangalore, 24th September 1992

EQUATIONS is a non-governmental organisation that campaigns for just, participatory and sustainable tourism. It is a working partner of the Ecumenical Coalition on Third World Tourism.

Tourism is the world's fastest growing industry and has widespread environmental, social and economic consequences.

World

• Between 1970 and 1990 tourism grew by nearly 300 per cent. It is expected to grow by half again before the end of the century. In 1991, an estimated 450 million tourists travelled internationally, or nearly eight per cent of the world's people.

• Tourism is the world's largest employer, employing 112 million people worldwide – that is 1 in every 15 employees. It pays US$540 billion annually in wages and salaries. [The World Travel and Tourism Council 1991]

• The tourism industry's turnover is expected to pass US$3.1 trillion in 1992 – equivalent to six per cent of the world's GNP.

• According to estimates, the tourism industry will be responsible for seven per cent of global capital investment in 1992.

• 80 per cent of all international travel is made up of nationals of just 20 countries.

• About 60 per cent of all international air travel is related to tourism.

North America

• Almost 400 million visits were made to North America's National Parks in 1991. [*Loved to Death*, World – BBC Magazine of Mankind, April 1992]

• Florida's coral reefs are thought to be worth $1.6 billion a year in tourist revenues. [*Coral Reefs – Valuable but Vulnerable*, WWF, September 1992, Gland, Switzerland]

• Recreational divers from the USA alone spend an annual $286 million in the Caribbean and Hawaii. [*Coral Reefs – Valuable but Vulnerable*, WWF, September 1992, Gland, Switzerland]

Antarctica

• Antarctica had around 3,500 tourists in 1990.

South-east Asia

• 60 per cent of Thailand's $4 billion a year tourism revenues flow out of the country. [National Institute for Development and Administration, Thailand, reported in *The Nation*, 13th March, 1990, Bangkok]

• In Thailand, tribal trekking has grown from a handful of hikers in the 1970s to more than 100,000 in 1988. [Tourism Authority of Thailand]

Australia

• Tourist-related activities around the Great Barrier Reef have increased six-fold since the early 1980s, and bring in $90 million each year. [*Coral Reefs – Valuable but Vulnerable*, WWF, September 1992, Gland, Switzerland]

• International tourism to Australia is projected to rise from 1.1 million to 6.5 million tourists by 2000. [Economist Intelligence Unit, Special Report No 2453, 1992]

Europe

• The Mediterranean region attracts over 100 million holiday makers every summer.

• Only some 30 per cent of sewage from coastal towns receives any treatment before being discharged into the Mediterranean.

• Over 500 Mediterranean plant species are threatened with extinction, and three quarters of European sand dunes on the coast between Gibraltar and Sicily have disappeared.

• The ski lifts that cover the Alps have the capacity to transport 1.5 million people per hour to 40,000 pistes. 50 million people visit the Alps annually. [*In Focus* No 5, Tourism Concern, London]

Unless otherwise indicated, all figures are taken from *Industry and Environment* Volume 15, No 3, United Nations Environment Programme, 1992.

As public concern mounts over the growing threats to our global environment and attention focuses on the need to manage our limited resources more sustainably, the operations of the world's major industries have come under increasing scrutiny. Yet one truly global and growing industry – tourism – has been largely ignored.

Beyond the Green Horizon – Principles for Sustainable Tourism has been commissioned by WWF UK to rectify this omission and to promote discussion. It is Tourism Concern's contribution to bringing tourism within the general debate on sustainable development. It is based on the principle advanced in 1987 by the Brundtland Report (*Our Common Future*) – "development that meets the needs of the present without compromising the ability of future generations to meet their own needs." Far from being in conflict with economic growth, the concept of sustainable development advocates the wise use and conservation of resources in order to maintain their long-term viability. It stresses that they cannot be conserved without addressing the broader range of problems which give rise to the unrelenting pressure for more development: widespread poverty, the mal-distribution of productive resources, inequalities in political representation and power, and the growth of a consumption-led society.

Tourism, perhaps more than any other activity, depends on quality human and natural environments and resources. Yet in general it is characterised by rapid, short-term development – the 'boom-and-bust' syndrome – which more often than not damages those very assets it seeks to exploit and, having wreaked havoc, simply moves off elsewhere. If it is not to contribute further to environmental degradation and destroy itself in the process, the tourism industry, like other businesses, must recognise its responsibility to the environment and learn how to become sustainable.

Beyond the Green Horizon aims to provide a tool for discussion about tourism, the environment and development. The first section sets out principles for sustainable tourism development and is aimed primarily at the tourism industry. The case studies which follow highlight various attempts to put such principles into practice. The book aims to further the debate which has already begun in the public arena and in some sectors of the tourism industry rather than to set absolute standards. As in other industries, the debate is an on-going one, the methodologies still being tried and tested, the results still uncertain.

One problem of definition immediately arises: what exactly is 'the tourism industry'? Is there any such monolithic thing as the title implies? In fact, what we call tourism really embraces a vast and diverse range of activities, from large-scale mass or package tours to small-scale, individually-tailored holidays; from internal domestic visits to family or friends, to international or intercontinental journeys, to business trips and 'sun sand and sea' recreational breaks; from activity, sports, nature, health, 'green' or alternative holidays, to culture or adventure. The tourism industry includes visits to beaches, coral reefs, countryside, ski-slopes, mountains, streams, islands, forests, deserts, national parks and wildernesses. Apart from such natural resources, tourism also depends on human resources: towns and cities, historical, cultural, religious, archaeological and heritage sites and traditions, as well as a vast array of economic, social, cultural, natural, technological and organisational assets. This book addresses tourism in all its various forms.

By all accounts the tourism industry is set to become the world's biggest, with an enormous economic potential. The UN estimates it will produce more revenue than the steel, car or even oil industries by the end of the decade. In 1991, the World Tourism Organisation[1] reported that world receipts from an estimated 450 million international tourist arrivals (compared to 60 million in 1960) amounted to $278 billion. A report for the American Express Company concludes that travel and tourism produces nearly 5.5 per cent of the world's total gross national product and generates $2.5 trillion in annual revenues overall. Tourism employs some 118 million people.[2] Naturally enough, the industry itself is the first to stress these potential benefits, particularly to destinations in need of hard currency; it is more reluctant to admit that, like other major industries, unplanned and uncontrolled tourism has severe environmental, social and economic impacts on the destination communities or localities. The damage caused by the over-development of tourism, from the Mediterranean to the Spanish Costas to resorts in Thailand or the mountains of Nepal, has been well publicised.

These impacts vary according to many factors, including the type and scale of the tourism enterprise, visitor numbers, and the nature of the destinations, their natural and built environments, facilities, infrastructure and overall stage of development, and importantly, their dependence on tourism for foreign currency, often to repay interest on international debts. Such destinations too often find themselves disadvantaged in dealing with the transnational companies which dominate the tourism industry.

The growth of tourism has coincided with increased leisure time and disposable income for many in the industrialised countries, who provide the bulk of the world's tourists. Europe generates 57 per cent of international tourist arrivals, with North America coming second with 16 per cent.[1] Thus the nature and scale of tourism is largely determined by the industry in the more affluent, tourism-generating centres, which is primarily motivated to see a return on its capital and investments, and which operates more usually for short-term benefit. The costs, in economic, environmental, social and cultural terms are paid by the less affluent in the tourism-receiving peripheries.

We do not argue that tourism should be stopped – this is unrealistic. We recognise that for many countries and regions, tourism presents a real alternative to other more obviously detrimental forms of development. However, as *Beyond the Green Horizon* indicates, if tourism is to be truly beneficial to all concerned, the owners of the industry, employees, tourists and 'hosts', and sustainable in the long-term, it must be ensured that resources are not over-consumed, that natural and human environments are protected, that tourism is integrated with other activities, that it provides real benefits to the local communities, often the bases of the tourism enterprise, that local people are involved and included in tourism planning and implementation, and that cultures and peoples are respected.

For tourism development to be sustainable requires due reference to the broader economic, political and social environment. It cannot be isolated from other forms of economic activity. Thus, tourism must take its place as part of programmes for integrated rural development of local economies, and should not dominate over wider programme objectives. Sustainable tourism emphasises the need to understand and respect the tourism resource base, to ensure a synergy of effort between relevant parties, involving cooperation, partnership, monitoring and research. In the absence of legislation the tourism industry must adhere to the highest international standards before punitive and restrictive action is imposed from the outside.

Above all, sustainable tourism involves an integrated approach to development and must not be simply a marketing ploy. There is undoubtedly a growth in 'alternative' or 'green' tourism catering to special interests in nature or culture, but the principles of sustainability must be implemented by the whole industry, including the mass market, not simply limited to a relatively expensive and specialised, small-scale, elite market.

The tourism industry must ensure that it conserves the resources on which it depends. As the chairman of American Airlines put it: "…it is in our self-interest to protect and preserve both the cultural and natural treasures of our world…" As the industry is surely aware, tourism itself is threatened by wider environmental problems – ozone depletion, deforestation, pollution, soil and beach erosion, rising sea levels. The tourism industry should therefore ally itself with others – government and non-government organisations, environmentalists, development agencies, pressure groups and local communities – if not take the lead in the global effort to achieve a sustainable society.

Sustainable tourism is... tourism and associated infrastructures that, both now and in the future:

- Operate within natural capacities for the regeneration and future productivity of natural resources;

- recognise the contribution that people and communities, customs and lifestyles, make to the tourism experience;

- accept that these people must have an equitable share in the economic benefits of tourism;

- are guided by the wishes of local people and communities in the host areas.

USING RESOURCES SUSTAINABLY

The conservation and sustainable use of resources — natural, social and cultural — is crucial and makes long-term business sense.

REDUCING OVER-CONSUMPTION AND WASTE

Reduction of over-consumption and waste avoids the costs of restoring long-term environmental damage and contributes to the quality of tourism.

MAINTAINING DIVERSITY

Maintaining and promoting natural, social and cultural diversity is essential for long-term sustainable tourism, and creates a resilient base for the industry.

INTEGRATING TOURISM INTO PLANNING

Tourism development which is integrated into a national and local strategic planning framework and which undertakes environmental impact assessments, increases the long-term viability of tourism.

SUPPORTING LOCAL ECONOMIES

Tourism that supports a wide range of local economic activities and which takes environmental costs and values into account, both protects those economies and avoids environmental damage.

INVOLVING LOCAL COMMUNITIES

The full involvement of local communities in the tourism sector not only benefits them and the environment in general but also improves the quality of the tourism experience.

CONSULTING STAKEHOLDERS AND THE PUBLIC

Consultation between the tourism industry and local communities, organisations and institutions is essential if they are to work alongside each other and resolve potential conflicts of interest.

TRAINING STAFF

Staff training which integrates sustainable tourism into work practices, along with recruitment of local personnel at all levels, improves the quality of the tourism product.

MARKETING TOURISM RESPONSIBLY

Marketing that provides tourists with full and responsible information increases respect for the natural, social and cultural environments of destination areas and enhances customer satisfaction.

UNDERTAKING RESEARCH

On-going research and monitoring by the industry using effective data collection and analysis is essential to help solve problems and to bring benefits to destinations, the industry and consumers.

USING RESOURCES SUSTAINABLY

The conservation and sustainable use of resources – natural, social and cultural – is crucial and makes long-term business sense

- All economic activities involve the use of resources, natural and human, many of which cannot be renewed, recycled or replaced.

- Sustainable development advocates leaving to future generations a stock of natural resources no less than that inherited by previous generations. This means preventing irreversible changes to environmental assets which have no substitute, preventing the loss of the ozone layer and living species, and damage to the essential functions of ecosystems such as tropical and primary forests, wetlands and coral reefs. It means accounting for services provided by natural environments, which are not 'free goods' but must be included in costing economic activities.

- The same principle also applies to human resources. Local cultures, traditions, livelihoods and the land on which they are based, need to be respected.

- The sustainable use, conservation and protection of these resources is increasingly recognised as vital to sound global management and makes good business sense. The International Chamber of Commerce[3] proposes that business enterprises should consider natural assets "in the same way as we would look at a viable business… getting as much as we can from [them]… without undermining the resource base."

Tourism and natural resources

- Tourism can be a powerful force for environmental preservation and protection. The last 40 years have seen a growth and expansion of national parks, wildlife sanctuaries and reserves designed to preserve endangered animal and plant species. Today there are over 5,000 worldwide[4], many of them dependent on income from tourism.

- While the growing market in nature and ecotourism reflects an increased public interest in the environment, this sector is small and limited in comparison to the mass and package tourism market. The rapid short-term and unplanned development of the latter has too often degraded the natural and human (social and cultural) resource base on which it depends.

- The tourism industry is increasingly adopting environmental policies. Disneyland in Florida, Center Parcs in the UK, the Sheraton and the Intercontinental Hotels Group, are addressing issues of waste disposal, recycling and water conservation. The Tourism Authority of Thailand emphasises the need to instil in tourists and the tourism industry "an understanding of the need to protect and conserve tourism resources…"[5]. The mission statement of the Wales Tourist Board includes principles of sustainability, while the English Tourist Board, the Countryside Commission and Rural Development Commission have recently published a guide to sustainable tourism[6]. For New Zealand, sustainable tourism means managing the environment in such a way that the "tourists, operators and host communities of the future" will enjoy the same resources as is possible today.[7]

- Despite such growing understanding and good intentions, much tourism development continues to damage the environment through over-construction, excessive visitor numbers, and vehicular and other types of pollution, diminishing the benefits for host societies, for tourists and ultimately for the industry itself.

- The installation of proper sewage systems in tourism projects would avoid water pollution, which is now almost universal. Examples include:
  – Thailand's Pattaya and Hua Hin coastal resorts where the waters of the Gulf of Thailand are no longer able to support shellfish.
  – The Philippines[8] where the unregulated building of coastal resorts has led to beach pollution.
  – Nepal where mountain streams have been polluted by human waste and litter left by trekkers.
  – Indonesia where sewage pollution has damaged Bali's coral reefs and eroded its protective beaches.
  – The French Pyrenees where the sewage of several thousand summer tourists[9] discharges directly into streams.
  – The Mediterranean, whose waters and beaches have been polluted by untreated human and other wastes and pollutants (such as oil from boating) from over 100 million annual holiday-makers.

- In all these cases, plant and animal life is threatened, the health of local people and tourists suffers and, unless the problems are addressed, the sites inevitably continue to decline.

- Problems of atmospheric pollution similarly need to be addressed: exhaust from the growing volume of tourist-carrying aircraft[10] and pollution produced by private cars, taxis and stationary tour buses,[11] the engines of which are left running to maintain air-conditioning, is affecting the quality of many tourist destinations. Traffic exhaust (in Europe's Alpine regions for example), not only contributes to damaging forests and wildlife, but destroys the very assets which attract tourists in the first place.

- The ill-considered construction of tourism facilities even damages areas such as national parks, whose prime purpose is environmental protection. In Phi-Phi National Park in South Thailand a protected limestone cliff was dynamited to build a hotel on supposedly common beachland. Extensive tree-clearing has been carried out in Thailand's Khao-Yai National Park to cut a main road, which is too wide for gibbons to cross.

- Ecological damage also results when the carrying-capacity of a national park has been exceeded:

  The National Parks in North America are being "loved to death",[12] by almost 400 million visitors in 1991 "trampling over the fragile habitat, ruining the flora with the pollution from their cars, scaring the animals, destroying the wilderness…" In Kenya, the central circuit of Amboseli National Park has been reduced to semi-desert by visitors' vehicles, while in the Maasai Mara, which receives 200,000 visitors a year, the construction of a large number of lodges outside the controlled area threatens to overload the system.[13]

- Specialist tourism development also damages the environment. The boom in golfing holidays, although promoted as environmentally friendly, often destroys natural grasslands. Millions of tons of earth may be removed, forests destroyed, mountains blown up, coastal areas bulldozed and valuable swampland drained in the process of laying a golf course. On Hong Kong's Lantau Island, for example, "over 5.2 million cubic feet of earth [were moved] from the peaks to the valleys…"

to construct the Discovery Bay Golf Club;[14] the laying of the Navathanee Golf Course near Bangkok has meant draining swampland and the use of vast amounts of fertilisers and pesticides;[15] in Hawaii, golf courses have been laid on ancient religious sites.[16] Further environmental damage results from the construction of clubhouses, hotels, shopping centres and related infrastructure for golfing tourists. In Thailand, 400 golf projects are in the planning stage, leaving aside the issue of whether all 400 are either necessary or viable. Those which are constructed must take environmental considerations into account.

- Proper regard also needs to be paid in the construction of hotels to avoid coastal erosion and subsequent damage to plants and animals. In the Mediterranean the breeding grounds of the Loggerhead Turtle have been destroyed. Coastal erosion through tourism development is common in Kenya, Goa and in the Philippines. Beach erosion in the Caribbean islands of Grenada and Antigua is so critical that costly sea defences have had to be built to protect hotel properties from collapse. And in Hawaii crowded beaches and commercial tour boating threaten the shoreline and coastal fishing.

- In Central and Eastern Europe there is a growing risk that tourism will be seen as a quick profit option at the expense of the last undisturbed habitats in Europe.

Tourism and human resources

- Although tourism development can provide employment and associated benefits to the local community, too often it has ignored their needs and rights. Several hundred Chhetri people had to be relocated from their traditional homeland when Lake Rara National Park in West Nepal was established. This led to a new wave of forest clearance elsewhere.

- The acquisition of 'choice locations' is vital to the tourist industry for the construction of hotels, beach resorts, condominiums, airports and golf courses. However, the local people are often dependent on the land and sea for a livelihood. Powerful tourism interests have from time to time managed to persuade, buy or

bribe governments and ministers and force people off their land. The story is repeated from Colombo (Sri Lanka) to Baguio (Philippines), from Bali (Indonesia) to Langkawi (Malaysia), from Honolulu to Hong Kong.

- Twenty years ago, the coast of Penang (Malaysia) was inhabited by fishing communities, and contained some of the country's most spectacular beaches. Today, the area is taken over with tourists and beach hotels.

  In 1984 seventy fishing families on the Malaysian island of Langkawi were evicted to make way for condominiums and hotels. In 1989, 29 shop owners were forced to move and their shops and houses knocked down because they were 'unsightly'. Recently, 45 families on Pangkor island were moved to make way for a runway to service tourists.[17]

- Conflicts over land for tourism development mean that families and communities who have lived for generations in such places as Hana, Maui, Maunawili and Waianae in Hawaii have been forced to leave because of a proposed golf course or hotel.

  Tourism development has played a major role in the destruction of ancient Hawaiian sacred sites. In 1991 a burial ground was excavated to make way for a condominium resort on the island of Kauai. Community opposition led to just one of the 22 acres being set aside to relocate the remains. At Honokahua, on the island of Maui, 1100 intact burial bundles were unearthed during a developer's excavations. Protests halted the development and a Burials Council has been formed to deal with the tourism-related problems.[18]

- Cultures can be revived through the interest of the wider tourist audience, leading to the restoration and protection of historic and cultural heritage. Country houses and castles in Britain, Mayan culture and cities in the Mundo Maya project in central America, and the remnants of Chinatown restored in Singapore are examples of such restoration.

- However, the sheer number of foreign visitors, particularly in small island resorts where the native population is often outnumbered, puts undoubted pressures on local cultures.

• Everywhere, in the attempt to adapt to tourist tastes, native dances have been uprooted from their time and place and distorted. In Malaysia, traditional Indian, Malay, Nonya/Baba wedding ceremonies – suitably abbreviated and choreographed – are staged in hotel lobbies; in Bali, sacred temple dances are offered as dinner entertainment in hotels.

Visitors to the Philippines may enjoy being treated to a 'typical Filipino dance' with Filipino dancers wearing mock Hawaiian grass skirts, clicking Spanish castanets and dancing who knows what… what this does to native culture is another matter.

• One of the more unhealthy aspects of tourism is its contribution to the sex industry. A high percentage of tourists to the Philippines, Thailand and Sri Lanka go not for the beauty of its temples or scenery but to gratify sexual appetites. Massage parlours, 'model' agencies, go-go bars, brothels, strip joints, sex cabarets and sex tours have all proliferated over the last two decades, and with the Aids scare, tourism has contributed to the growth in child prostitution as clients look for virgins. In Central and Eastern Europe, the threat of cities, in particular Prague, becoming centres for sex tourism is high.

RECOMMENDATIONS

The tourism industry should:

• **Prevent damage to environmental resources, natural and human.**

• **Act as a force for conservation.**

• **Develop and implement sound environmental policies in all areas of tourism.**

• **Install appropriate systems for minimising water and atmospheric pollution from tourism developments.**

• **Develop and implement sustainable transport policies, efficient public transport – and walking and cycling – to enhance and protect the environment.**

• **Adhere to the Precautionary Principle in all its operations and new developments.**

• **Research and establish the carrying-capacity of a destination and then operate within the limits that this sets, respecting the Precautionary Principle.**

• **Respect the needs and rights of local people.**

• **Protect and support the cultural and historical heritage of peoples worldwide.**

• **Carry out its practices in a responsible and ethical manner.**

• **Actively discourage the growth of exploitative sex tourism.**

REDUCING OVER-CONSUMPTION AND WASTE

Reduction of over-consumption and waste avoids the costs of restoring long-term environmental damage and contributes to the quality of tourism

- It is becoming increasingly recognised that over-consumption is detrimental to our global environment and inconsistent with long-term sustainable development. This pattern of consumption is characteristic of the developed industrialised countries but is rapidly spreading worldwide as 'Western' or 'Northern' lifestyles are presented as a goal to which to aspire.

- Projects which have been initiated without Environmental Impact Assessments (EIAs), or where recommendations from such assessments have not been implemented, have led to the wasteful and unnecessary consumption of environmental and other resources. This has resulted in pollution and social and cultural disruption.

- Waste resulting from such projects is often neglected or mismanaged, leading to long-term environmental degradation.

- The restoration of damage caused by unplanned or ill-planned projects, particularly by those in the private sector, is often left to other, public sector bodies to carry out. Many companies are now recognising the inherent justice of the 'polluter-pays' principle.

Tourism and consumption

- The over-consumption of natural and other resources in tourism, such as the excessive use of water, wood or food, is not only damaging to the local environment but is incompatible with the long-term sustainability of the industry.

- Tourism has affected the consumption of water in resorts worldwide: swimming pools in luxury hotels, running showers and taps and constant lawn sprinklers, aggravate water shortages. Examples include hotels (mostly foreign-owned) on the Gambian coast, where many local inhabitants still have to raise water from hand dug wells; Goa, where the supply of water to tourist hotels has actively reduced its availability to local people; and Thailand where despite a severe water shortage an estimated 3,000 cubic meters of water are used daily on one golf course alone.

- Demand from tourists has also contributed damage to forests and woodlands:

In Nepal, 400,000 hectares of forest are cleared each year. A Nepalese government report of 1977 estimated that tourist demand for fuelwood had increased deforestation by ten per cent. The total daily wood consumption by and on behalf of each trekker equals the amount used by a Nepalese family of five for a week.[19] Forest is cleared each year to construct hotels, lodges and furniture and to provide fuel for cooking, hot showers and campfires. This has led to increased risks of landslides and floods.

- In the Gambia, electricity consumption in tourist hotels for lighting and air-conditioning necessitates the use of wood-burning stoves in nearby shanty towns where the electricity supply often fails.

- Tourists' demand for seafood has added to the over-exploitation of marine wildlife, lobster and conch in the Caribbean, adding to the worldwide problem of over-fishing which, due to modern technology, has already increased by 500 per cent over the last 40 years.[20]

- In areas where certain resources are plentiful for both local inhabitants and tourists, imports are unnecessary, wasteful and non cost-effective. Furthermore, local sourcing can benefit the tourism industry in terms of local goodwill and special local character. These gains in turn offset any direct increase in costs that would be avoided by importing goods.

An EC-funded hotel construction project in Western Samoa uses traditional designs and techniques and only imports materials where local substitutes cannot be produced economically. The project is based on the ownership of the hotel sites by the local villagers, the employment of local people and the use of local agricultural produce for consumption by tourists.[21]

- Where suitable local sources are inadequate for tourists' comforts which are perceived as essential, i.e. sophisticated hotel fittings or imported food and drink, deficiencies can be met by encouraging local enterprises. Where imports are regarded as vital they should be purchased as far as possible through local agencies.

- Some materials may have to be imported where local resources are scant. For example, the lack of wood due to inadequate forestation means that timber has to be imported into the Orkney and Shetland Islands. Although a certain amount of trade can be beneficial, emphasis should rather be placed on developing sustainable indigenous replacements. In Tonga, for example, a project to promote women's handicraft production for the tourism market is encouraging wood replantation in order to sustain the supply of raw material for production.

Tourism and waste

- The tourism industry should take waste disposal costs into account as part of purchase. In many countries such costs are rising rapidly and the agreement of a tourism supplier to develop recycling facilities and to accept used products for this purpose could have cost benefits that are not immediately apparent to those with an ingrained lowest cash cost approach.

- Companies are increasingly recognising their responsibilities in this regard, which is especially important where local infrastructure is inadequate or non-existent:

The policy statement of the Inter-Continental Hotels Group includes a commitment to a programme which "efficiently manages and minimises our waste production, to the benefit of our environment." Although it might not always be possible to implement more elaborate programmes, particularly in underdeveloped countries due to the lack of infrastructure, the Inter-Continental Hotels statement maintains that it is still "invariably possible to take action benefiting the environment" and to apply the general philosophy.

- The indirect impacts of waste are more difficult to control: aqueous wastes from adjacent resorts or increased atmospheric emissions, for example from aircraft or motorised traffic, may leave their impact on locations far removed from their origins. Although it may be hard to establish a precise source-effect relationship, such impacts must be taken into account.

- Under some conditions waste can be of value to the local economy. Many developed economies have much to learn from the reuse and recycling of waste, tourist-related or otherwise, in poorer areas. In the long-term, the tourism industry would benefit from investigating and encouraging appropriate recycling schemes.

In the South Peruvian Amazon, traditional-style lodges have been constructed to attract tourists to the jungle region. However, none of the lodges have addressed the question of waste disposal, which is either burned or dumped in pits, but not removed from the area. The human waste drains into crude cesspits and ultimately into rivers. The possibility of recycling or tapping it as an energy source has so far not been investigated.[22]

• Problems also arise where tourism is promoted and provided by commercial interests which have no responsibility for dealing with its effects.

Restoring damage

• Waste and pollution arising from tourist developments which contribute only marginally to the local economy are often left to local authorities to deal with. This is particularly true where tourism services such as food, transport and entertainment are largely self-contained or are imported from elsewhere.

• The deterioration of many Mediterranean beach resorts such as Benidorm or Majorca has forced tour companies to take positive remedial action in order to save their investment. Benidorm now has some of the cleanest beaches in the Mediterranean, while the current initiative on Majorca, supported by the International Federation of Tour Operators, aims to produce a model balance between social, economic and environmental demands by identifying maximum sustainable tourism flow.

• Proper planning, together with comprehensive EIAs, could have prevented such damage in the first place and avoided the subsequent costs to the industry. As the 'polluter-pays' principle becomes internationally accepted, it is in the interests of any industry to ensure that such problems are avoided through proper planning and implementation.

RECOMMENDATIONS

The tourism industry should:

• **Reduce consumption and promote the reduction of inappropriate consumption by its customers.**

• **Use local resources in preference to imports, but in an appropriate and sustainable manner.**

• **Only import goods when absolutely necessary, and ensure these are imported through local agencies and enterprises.**

• **Reduce waste.**

• **Ensure the safe disposal of waste produced from its tourism facilities.**

• **Implement waste disposal facilities, including support for local infrastructure where this is inadequate.**

• **Recycle waste to the benefit of the tourism industry and of the local community, where waste cannot be reduced.**

• **Invest in appropriate recycling schemes.**

• **Take responsibility for restoring damage arising from tourism projects.**

• **Avoid damage through proper pre-planning and constant monitoring.**

3

MAINTAINING DIVERSITY

Maintaining and promoting natural, social and cultural diversity is essential for long-term sustainable tourism, and creates a resilient base for the industry

Diversity

- Diversity in natural, cultural and social environments is a strength which provides resilience to shocks and stress. It is also vital in order to avoid over-dependency on one or a few bases of life support.

- Natural environments in particular are characterised by diversity, but irreversible ecological destruction has taken place on a massive scale. It is estimated that within the next 50 years one quarter of all animal species will be extinct. To date many vital wetlands, 80 per cent of all coral reefs and half the planet's original forests have been lost.[23]

- Sustainable development advocates leaving to future generations a diversity of wealth – human and natural – no less than that inherited by previous generations. Recognising that change in biological, cultural and economic environments is an inevitable consequence of any kind of development, this means exploiting the various functions of the environment within its carrying-capacity while avoiding serious and irreversible damage.

- The World Conservation Strategy (1980) stressed the need to preserve genetic diversity. Since then the aim has broadened to include the diversity of socio-economic and political structures and cultures.

- The growth of environmental and conservation organisations and campaigns[24] to protect indigenous peoples, tropical forests or species, shows the increasing public concern for preserving diversity.

Tourism and natural diversity

- Diversity underpins much of the tourism industry, whether landscape, wildlife or culture. A rich and varied environment different from their own is often an important factor in determining tourists' choice of destinations – an interest which tour operators have marketed with varying degrees of sensitivity. However, the rapid and uncontrolled over-development of tourism has endangered and ultimately destroyed those very assets on which it depends, affecting benefits for hosts, tourists and the industry alike.

- Tourism can undoubtedly be a powerful force for maintaining natural diversity. National parks, nature reserves and sanctuaries, largely supported by income from tourism, all contribute to the protection of diversity. Projects such as the 'Programme for Belize' seek to maintain and encourage diversity by encouraging visitors and tourists to help protect the natural environment. However, problems arise from the very success of these enterprises:

The Galapagos Islands of Ecuador were declared a 'universal natural heritage of humanity' by UNESCO in 1978. Problems directly attributable to tourism, despite visitor controls, include disruption to the albatross, sea lions, marine turtles (which have swallowed plastic bags thinking them to be jellyfish), black coral (the islands' prime souvenir), tourists feeding animals and path erosion.[25]

In 1990, Antarctica had around 3,500 tourists but this number is set to increase with the construction of an airfield at Rothera scientific station.[26] The dangers of the uncontrolled development of the world's last great reserve of natural resources were recognised in the 1991 Environmental Protocol which imposed a 50-year ban on mining and regulations on pollution control, wildlife protection and tourism in the area.[27]

- Diversity is threatened by the construction of extensive facilities for tourism, especially where development occurs without prior regard to an area's special features. In the Caribbean islands, tourism facilities are partly to blame for destroying the nesting areas of at least seven types of turtle.[28] In the French Alps the black grouse is threatened by the rapid development of winter tourism.[29] In the Philippines' island of Cebu, regarded as a classic case of unsustainable development, five coral islands have totally disappeared, partly due to the mining of coral for building tourism structures, such as the main terminal of Cebu City airport.[30] In Bulgaria skiing developments threaten mountain ecology in Pirini National Park. Such destruction, apart from being unacceptable from a global perspective, can only be detrimental to the long term sustainability of tourism enterprises.

Tourism and social diversity

- Social diversity, like natural diversity, is one of the tourism industry's major resources. As such, it is in the industry's interest to protect it. Indeed, when tourism development is both sustainable and part and parcel of a community's activities, it can underpin the diversity of fragile societies, providing employment to areas which, for reasons of accessibility, environment, natural resources and/or politics, are peripheral. One example of a practical initiative is the Mid-Wales Festival of the Countryside, a federated programme of 600 rural events and activities which aims to combine tourism with environmental education and rural development.[31]

- However, rapid and uncontrolled development of major tourism enterprises can destroy the diversity of local and regional social structures, particularly when they are introduced from outside the region or country and are neither known, understood nor controlled by the local community.

- The diversity of local or regional social systems and ecosystems is also reduced when traditional occupations, such as fishing and agriculture, are neglected in favour of jobs in tourism, which becomes the region's predominant 'monoculture'. As work patterns are replaced by unfamiliar and often inappropriate new ones, old social patterns are disrupted and cooperation is replaced by competition. The resulting social tensions can benefit neither the local population nor the tourism product itself.

- Tourism also contributes to the process of urbanisation, which causes the social dislocation of rural or coastal communities, and which is particularly marked when local people have little or no say in development decisions affecting their lives.

- Local people, particularly the young, are often attracted to the glamorous lifestyle and conspicuous consumption associated with tourism. This may be inappropriate to local social or economic conditions and contribute to conflicts and divisions with elders and parents.

- Tourism has introduced or aggravated social problems, such as drug abuse, alcoholism, crime and prostitution, often with severe negative social effects.

In the Galapagos Islands, competition between the wealthier tourism sector and others is producing direct cultural conflict, aggravated by the fact that most of the tourism labour force is brought in from mainland Ecuador. Newcomers now outnumber those who grew up with and learned to value the special, fragile nature of the islands.[32]

Tourism and cultural diversity

- Cultural diversity forms part of the tourism industry's primary assets and, arguably, is what many tourists travel to find, so it should be fostered and protected.

- Tourism can strengthen a society's culture by providing employment at local level and an incentive for young people to stay, rather than emigrate in search of work. Traditional culture is often encouraged by being performed for the wider tourist audience.

- But much cultural diversity is lost when local people and their culture become degraded as part of the 'product' sold to tourists. It is further eroded by the demands of tour operators for standardisation to satisfy tourists' perceived needs – for example, familiar cuisine such as 'an English breakfast'. Resorts worldwide are standardised to provide tourists with facilities conforming to, or even better than, those left at home, complete with modern amenities and the opportunity to spend as much as possible in shops and tourist experiences. It becomes hard to tell whether one is in Benidorm, Phuket, Florida or Waikiki, since even the garden plants look the same! Such standardisation strips a community of its individuality and ultimately of its uniqueness as a tourist destination.

- Cultural diversity is further eroded by local communities having to adapt their own culture to serve tourists' needs, often entailing the adoption of a 'service' mentality. Local people are expected to offer smiling hospitality, even when they may have been alienated from their land and traditional livelihoods and when the scale and type of tourism is far from conducive to genuine hospitality. The mass importation of foreign cultures, usually marked by conspicuous consumption, does little to further the 'mutual understanding' so often advocated by tourism developers. Appropriate and sustainable tourism, on the other hand, may offer such opportunities and thus improve the tourism experience for all concerned.

RECOMMENDATIONS

The tourism industry should:

- **Respect the natural, social and cultural diversity of destination areas.**

- **Ensure a pace, scale and type of development which protects rather than destroys diversity, local culture and communities.**

- **Prevent the destruction of natural diversity by respecting each area's carrying-capacity, taking steps to establish carrying-capacities and adopting the Precautionary Principle.**

- **Monitor the impact of tourism activities on the flora and fauna of a destination area.**

- **Encourage social and economic diversity by integrating tourism within the activities of a local community and with their full participation.**

- **Prevent viable traditional occupations from being displaced by a tourism monoculture.**

- **Actively discourage forms of tourism which cause or contribute to social problems.**

- **Foster genuine cultural tourism that does not reduce the host culture to a commodity.**

- **Promote a region's unique features, rather than impose blanket standardisation.**

- **Ensure that the scale, pace and type of tourism is such as to foster genuine hospitality and mutual understanding.**

- **Promote tourism in tune with local culture, welfare and development aspirations.**

INTEGRATING TOURISM INTO PLANNING

Tourism development which is integrated into a national and local strategic planning framework and which undertakes environmental impact assessments, increases the long-term viability of tourism

- Conflicts of interest, the over-use of resources and over-dependency can be avoided or minimised by the integration of any one sector with other sectors. Such integrated development rests on two principles: strategic long term planning and environmental impact assessment (EIA).

- A *strategic planning framework* provides a context for evaluating the short, medium and long-term impacts of development on local and regional environmental, economic and social conditions.

- *Environmental impact assessment*, undertaken in the planning and implementation stages of a project, is essential in order to minimise disruption to natural, social and economic environments.

- EIAs are still being developed and tested. However, within the European Community, the directive of 1985[33] stipulates that EIAs should include a project's direct and indirect impact on human beings, flora and fauna, soil, water, air, climate and landscape the interaction between these factors and material assets and cultural heritage. A public or private developer must submit relevant information to a competent authority for consent for a project.

Tourism and strategic planning

- When tourism development is an integral part of a national plan which considers development and environmental management as a whole, it results in maximum long-term rather than short-term benefits for national and local economies and for the industry.

- Such properly planned tourism enhances values placed on environmental assets, provides incentives for conserving threatened species and ecosystems, and brings improvements to local communities. This in turn leads to a better quality tourism product.

- However, in practice, tourism development is rarely balanced with other sectors, such as local industry and agriculture, which can provide invaluable resources in the form of equipment, transportation, foodstuffs etc. These sectors can in turn benefit from the tourism market.

- Where tourism is not integrated with other sectors and balanced through strategic planning, it can result in uncontrolled and rapid expansion, which often has disastrous consequences, including environmental effects such as surface erosion of walking areas, the visual blight of concrete jungles, pollution of bathing water and damage to flora and fauna.

- Particular problems arise when the local economy is relatively fragile and the prospect of even low-level, short-term employment is seductive – or when development is promoted without regard to the infrastructural costs to the community, the effect on local agriculture, land prices and housing markets.

- Even where the importance of integrated planning is understood, the time taken to produce an overall plan may mean that individual initiatives are taking place unchecked. The industry may then be subject to governmental measures, such as the introduction of temporary freezing – the 'white zone' scheme in Cyprus – while policy is being worked out.

Tourism and environmental impact assessments (EIAs)

- In tourism, EIAs are imperative in order to assess whether the scale or type of tourist development is appropriate, and whether it will bring net benefits to the area, region or country. In short, whether it is sustainable or not.

- Within the EC, the 1985 directive includes a number of tourism projects specifically recommended for EIAs: ski-lifts and cable-cars, the construction of roads, harbours and airfields, yacht marinas, holiday villages and hotel complexes.

- To date, EIAs have been successfully carried out and implemented mainly in 'eco-tourism' projects, such as Manu Lodge in Manu National Park in Peru, where small groups of tourists stay in accommodation built in keeping with the local environments. Within Europe, EIAs have also been undertaken by mainstream tourist enterprises, such as Center Parcs and EuroDisney in France, illustrating a growing awareness on the part of

the mass tourism industry. EIAs for tourism development can and should be reproduced elsewhere.

- Outside Europe, EIAs have been carried out in countries such as New Zealand, Seychelles and Australia.

The pace of growth in international tourism to Australia, from 1.1m to an anticipated 6.5m by 2000, has prompted the Australian Tourist Commission to call for mandatory EIAs of tourism developments and greater public scrutiny to avoid "partial reporting" by assessors. Projects will have to be evaluated within the context of the whole region, and consideration of cultural and social impacts, change in style and pace of life, crime, local employment and living conditions. A national tourism strategy, ensuring minimum standards of environmental management would prevent such environmentally damaging schemes as the high-density, high-rise holiday apartments along Queensland's Gold Coast.[34]

- EIAs are important in order to make a comprehensive assessment of the environmental, social, cultural and economic impacts of tourism. They assess economic benefits and disadvantages, employment creation and displacement, environmental improvement and interference, cultural enhancement and disruption.

- Such impact assessments also take into account possible conflicts of interest between various groups: host communities, visitors, national and regional governments and agencies, local and foreign tourism operators, travel and hotel companies. For example, the EIAs being carried out in the field of airport development by the International Air Transport Association (IATA) and Airfields Environment Federation include social and economic factors, and allow for different opinions on atmospheric emissions, noise and visual impact.

- The airports project also puts tourism development into a wider perspective by anticipating the 'domino effect' of solving one problem of congestion by taking land for roads or accommodation. Such an integrated approach is essential for sustainable long-term development. On the other hand, the individual assessments for new hotel construction in St Lucia are of limited value since they have not considered the wider impacts of all the hotels on the island's cultural and environmental infrastructure.

• Although EIAs may entail greater initial investment by the industry, tourism enterprises which are more appropriate and sustainable will increase long-term benefits to all concerned. This may require the use of data-gathering and processing technology. The introduction of such technology in developing countries should be supported.

The Belize government has brought scientists into its tourism planning process. Marine biologists are preparing a coastal zone management plan to identify areas for protection and for tourism, including fishing zones and critical habitats, such as the mangroves outside Belize City. Working with them is the Geography Department of Edinburgh University which is mapping the mangroves in order to control and coordinate development for tourism, urban expansion, fisheries, coastal protection and timber use. LandSat satellite imagery is used to produce regular up-dated pictures of large areas at low cost (£3,000 per 150 sq km) – cheaper than traditional aerial photos. These, combined with field work, provide vegetation maps for the whole country. The maps generated by satellite imagery are then transferred onto a Geographical Information System (GIS). GIS superimposes several layers of data – such as access (roads, canals), the distribution of habitats, nesting sites etc. – in order to build up detailed information on how variables interrelate. This assists in the selection of areas most suitable for tourism. Such state-of-the-art technology enables scientists to test development strategies on the computer without turning over a single stone.[35]

• Without EIAs the rapid and unplanned tourism characteristic of present-day development often distorts local economies, causes major pollution and severely erodes local cultures and environments. Moderate, planned tourism, on the other hand, is more likely to enhance local standards of living. Impact assessments should, therefore, include the positive contribution which appropriate tourism can make.

RECOMMENDATIONS

The tourism industry should:

• Take into account both the immediate and future needs of hosts and tourists.

• Integrate all economic, environmental, social, and cultural aspects of the local area in planning.

• Respect local, regional and national policy in other sectors – industry, agriculture, land-use, housing and welfare.

• Consider alternative strategies for development and options for land-use that take environmental imperatives into account.

• Minimise environmental, social and cultural damage to host communities by carrying out comprehensive environmental impact assessments in consultation with local people and all relevant authorities.

• Continue to monitor positive and negative environmental and other impacts of the industry's activities prior to and during development.

• Develop and introduce methodologies for improving environmental impact assessments undertaken by the industry.

• Recognise that a pace of development in concert with local situations will provide time to properly plan, develop and monitor projects for long-term benefits.

SUPPORTING LOCAL ECONOMIES

Tourism that supports a wide range of local economic activities and which takes environmental costs and values into account, both protects those economies and avoids environmental damage

- Economic growth, as conventionally measured by Gross National Product (GNP) and calculated from the market price of goods and services, excludes non-marketed goods and informal activities and has treated environmental services and resources as 'free goods'. Such failure to cost environmental values has usually meant trade-offs in favour of unlimited growth to the detriment of the environment.

- Sustainable development, on the other hand, aims at improving people's overall satisfaction and welfare while maintaining and improving the environment. This means taking its vital economic functions into account and incorporating environmental quality into investment decisions – 'ecological accounting'. It also means integrating environmental values into traditional cost-benefit analyses (CBAs). Such CBAs have been used to show the monetary value of forest conservation in Cameroon and Nigeria.[36/37]

- Central to sustainable economic development is the avoidance of dependency on a narrow economic base and the promotion of economic diversity. It also entails restructuring market systems to account not only for environmental services but also the wider social costs of production.

- The business community is increasingly taking the environment into consideration in response to public opinion. Surveys within the European Community regularly show concern for the environment ranking second to unemployment.

Tourism and environmental accounting

- Where tourism depends directly on the quality of the environment the industry has recognised its interest in maintaining and improving standards: cleaner beaches, protected wetlands and coral reefs from Belize to Florida, entrance fees and tourist taxes, income from hunting licenses, elephant and rhinoceros conservation projects in Zambia and Zimbabwe, game reserves in Kenya – all highlight the direct monetary value of the environment. Such projects return much tourism revenue to conservation, and by providing local communities with an income, prevent the poaching of protected species or land misuse, at the same time stimulating other sectors of the local economy, such as agriculture, construction and handicrafts.

- However, the tourism industry has been less willing to recognise the value of the environment when it comes to those enterprises which are not so obviously dependent on it. Here the pursuit appears to be more for rapid, short-term economic returns rather than long-term economic development or benefits to the environment and to host communities. This results in overdeveloped tourist sites established without adequate infrastructure, environmental auditing or regard to carrying-capacity, leading to environmental degradation and ultimately to their own non-viability. When this happens tourism companies may be able to simply move elsewhere – with devastating economic impact on those countries or regions which depend on them for foreign currency. But such practices are under increasing scrutiny and criticism and hardly in the industry's ultimate interests.

Tourism, economic diversity and dependency

- Tourism can underpin economic diversification by stimulating activity in peripheral areas. Properly planned investment in infrastructure, such as roads, power and water supply, sewage and communications, can serve non-tourism development while also reinforcing and encouraging the tourism industry.

- When tourism is introduced into areas with non-diverse economies, which may most wish to encourage tourism, it may be problematic to integrate it within an economic structure that cannot cater for more than the simplest form of tourism. In such cases certain forms of tourism, such as mass package holidays, are inappropriate. Greater benefits for hosts, tourists and the industry alike will be gained from the development of more appropriate forms of tourism which can stimulate new, diverse and sustainable forms of economic activity.

The Laona Project in Cyprus aims to introduce appropriate tourism to the unspoilt Akamas Peninsula by restoring villages to provide accommodation for high-quality tourism

in preference to five-star beach resort hotels, benefiting the local community and protecting the green and loggerhead turtles of the Akamas.[38]

- Tourism as a form of economic diversification can also help maintain threatened lifestyles such as farming in the UK:

It is estimated that 1,000 people are leaving the land in Britain every month. Many of those who remain can only do so by diversifying and introducing tourism and recreation facilities: golf courses, horse riding stables, bed and breakfast accommodation or caravan sites. Such activities can support farmers' incomes.[39/40]

- Where activities such as farming and crafts already exist, they must not be allowed to decline in favour of tourism but help improve and sustain it. Where agriculture is neglected and farm land sold off to tourism enterprises, such as in the Thai resorts of Phuket and Ko Samui, necessities such as food, transport and goods must be imported. Economic diversity is essential in order to minimise hard currency expenditure on imports, while the larger and more diverse the economic base, the less a destination needs to import and the less the 'leakage' of foreign currency.

- When concentrated in a small area of a country or in the hands of a few people, tourism can aggravate both regional and social disparities in development. Flourishing employment, living standards and consumption levels for some, added to the unequal distribution of benefits to a portion of the population, can contribute to social tensions and hostility, as on some Caribbean islands. This, in turn, will have a negative effect on the tourism industry.

Diversification can be promoted by the distribution of tourism earnings across a destination country. Examples include the development of rural areas, such as Gites de France, public sector financial support for some high quality hotels in rural areas in Spain, increasing local employment and decreasing migration, and in Kenya the construction, by African Tours and Hotels, of hotels in areas which were not previously on the tourist circuit, stimulating development in lower income areas.

- Tourism earnings can also be distributed through encouraging income-generating schemes and small businesses which will benefit from wider tourism activity. Such enterprises, for example, the agro-tourist cooperatives run by women in Greek villages, not only provide an independent source of income, but also enhanced status and self-determination. Other projects include encouraging linkages between tourism and agriculture, as in Fiji, or stimulating local handicrafts, as on the South Pacific islands of Kiribati and Tonga, with a wood replantation project to sustain a supply of raw materials.[41]

- Economic diversification is particularly important since tourism is a notoriously volatile 'boom and bust' activity, affected by factors such as international money markets, recession, political instability, oil prices, consumer tastes and marketing by large transnational corporations in tourism-generating countries. Egypt witnessed an 80 per cent drop in tourism the year of the Gulf War. The US bombing of Libya led to a drop in tourism across Europe. Civil unrest in Fiji similarly affected tourist numbers.

- Dependence on such an unstable industry is risky, particularly for those developing countries for which it is a single industry needed to bring in essential hard currency. The strategy can work, resorts like Blackpool in the UK, although feeling the effects of the current recession, have subsisted successfully for years on such a narrow base. But it puts the local community at the mercy of swings in fashion and of the interests of particular tour operators.

- Much tourist expenditure fails to reach the destination country when package tourists pay at source for accommodation and travel on foreign airlines. Some developing destinations – such as Malaysia, India and Thailand – have increased national earnings by providing competitive air transport, despite problems of protectionism. Further shares go to foreign intermediaries, such as the tour operators, whose strong bargaining position enables them to negotiate advantageous contractual terms with destination countries. A study by the UN Centre on

Transnational Corporations found that terms of contract provided large benefits to transnational corporations relative to destination countries.[42]

- While much of the profits are lost through imports or repatriation, the costs of expensive infrastructure used mainly by tourists and of environmental damage, usually fall to the host country. For example, for every American tourist dollar brought into the Bahamas it is estimated that at least 80 cents goes straight back out again to pay for imported foodstuffs.[43] The costs of tourism infrastructure may be met by taxes paid by the local population which often benefits only marginally from it. The tourism industry must ensure that the local population is not solely responsible for financing the tourism infrastructure and the damage that tourists cause.

Taxation policies, such as airport tax in Kenya, hotel tax in Guatemala, motorway toll tax in Italy, ensure that tourists contribute part of the cost of infrastructure provision and maintenance. Kenya Wildlife Service, for example, has increased entry charges for foreign tourists to national game parks and reserves. The income goes towards conservation and to improving the living standard of populations in or near the reserves.

RECOMMENDATIONS

The tourism industry should:

- Take responsibility for maintaining and improving the environment where this is a direct resource.

- Ensure that environmental costs are taken into account in all tourism projects.

- Integrate environmental considerations into all economic decisions.

- Operate within the limits set by local appropriate infrastructure and carrying-capacity.

- Undertake full and regular environmental audits of every tourism project.

- Underpin economic diversity by developing tourism infrastructures that also benefit wider interests.

- Ensure that the type and scale of tourism is appropriate to local conditions.

- Prevent over-exploitation of individual locations.

- Support local income generation and small business enterprises.

- Support the economies of destination countries by maximising retention of tourist revenues within their economies.

- Invest in environmental protection technologies and in restoration of existing damage to the environment in relation to tourism.

6

INVOLVING LOCAL COMMUNITIES

The full involvement of local communities in the tourism sector not only benefits them and the environment in general but also improves the quality of the tourism experience

- Projects imposed from outside and motivated by the pursuit of rapid economic growth often override local needs, conditions and resources, and result in unacceptable environmental, social and cultural costs.

- Local involvement is crucial to sustainable and appropriate development which meets the needs of local people and safeguards their natural and cultural environments. To this end a local development strategy is essential, especially in disadvantaged areas and/or countries.

- Schemes such as the EC-funded Local Employment Development Action (LEDA), aim to provide employment in disadvantaged areas through partnerships between business, local government, labour organisations, voluntary and community groups, and to foster greater understanding of local conditions, ways of problem-solving and mobilising and administering resources.[44]

- Likewise, the Prince of Wales Business Trust proposes coordination between business, government and non-governmental organisations in order to foster sustainable development that benefits the local as well as the business community. Local involvement makes a community more supportive, confident and productive, with a sense of pride and commitment to the future.

- Educational programmes that prepare people for participation in the process of defining and implementing development strategies that are socially and environmentally sensitive are vital. This is the focus of WWF's CADISPA project (Conservation and Development in Sparsely Populated Areas). In all of the current project areas (Scotland, Portugal, Spain, Italy, Greece) tourism is a major consideration.

Tourism and local involvement

- Local involvement is essential to tourism: local peoples, their culture, environment, way of life and traditions, are important factors which attract tourists to a location. The needs and aspirations of local peoples must therefore be fully supported.

- Carefully developed tourism can provide real economic, environmental and cultural benefits to the community.

In turn, genuine community involvement can enrich the tourism experience and product.

• When a community is involved in the direction of tourism development it is more likely to become an active partner and to provide checks and balances since it has a particular stake in the region and commitment to environmental quality. The long-term viability of tourism depends on the support and involvement of the local community.

• Local involvement in tourism projects has been successful in the community-led Locus project in Aberfeldy in the Scottish Highlands, the Gites system in France, the paradores in Spain and farm holidays in Scandinavian countries.

Those involved in the Mid-Wales Festival of the Countryside constitute a loose 'family' which identifies with the overall initiative. The perceived strengths of the participants include experience, professionalism and a good understanding and love of their area or subject, which they use to promote a better understanding by visitors.[45]

• It has been argued that tourism contributes to local development by providing destination countries with foreign exchange and employment. However, it is increasingly realised that such benefits do not automatically 'trickle down' to all levels of society. There is little evidence that increased tourism to India, Indonesia, Thailand or Malaysia during their 'Visit' years has filtered through to alleviate poverty. Genuine local involvement would go some way to doing so, at the same time improving the long-term prospects of the tourism product.

The Kenya Wildlife Service has launched a programme of environmental reforms which aims to ensure that landowners outside the national parks benefit from wildlife tourism based on animal watching, game bird shooting and game cropping (for the restaurant business). The ban on sport hunting may be lifted only with proper management and the agreement of the Kenyan people.[46]

• Local involvement means more than employment in the usual low-paid, seasonal menial and service jobs,

such as waiters, chambermaids and gardeners. Higher status and better paid management jobs, often filled by expatriate staff, should be made available to local people whose special local knowledge and expertise would add invaluable quality to the tourism experience.

• Local involvement, through encouraging the local ownership of craft and cottage industries, guiding services, transportation and accommodation, shops and restaurants, would prevent the leakage of foreign currency and benefit both host community and tourists alike. However, ownership by a local elite will not ensure the equitable distribution of benefits or environmental accountability.

• The promotion of home-based bed-and-breakfast accommodation or farmhouse holidays is a further encouragement to local involvement and provides tourists with an enriching alternative to the mass market.

• Small-scale, community-led projects can contribute significantly to raising living standards. However, commercial success and the need to meet demands makes it hard to prevent them evolving into large-scale enterprises. On the other hand, the infrastructure of mass tourism can in turn lead to successful small projects involving local people (see case study on the Lower Casamance, Senegal).

• A gradual pace of tourism development gives local people time to adjust to new environmental, social and economic conditions and helps prevent the adverse results of rapid uncontrolled ventures. The involvement of local people in determining their own development would prevent conflicts that inevitably affect the sustainability of tourism.

Local people's homelands in Puerto Galera on Mindoro Island and Boracay in the Philippines were targeted by the Marcos government as luxury resorts for tourists. The residents united against these plans and managed, to a great extent, to maintain local control over tourism development. Although the communities now participate in the development plans they still need to be vigilant in order to defend their involvement in their own 'backyard tourism'.[47]

• While the creation of national parks, marine and nature reserves, or tourist enclaves on beaches, pasture or agricultural land, may protect endangered species and habitats, they can marginalise local communities and deprive them of traditional livelihoods.

Tourists on safari in Tanzania may be aware of the need to conserve wild species, but few realise the impact of conservation on local people. The Ngorongoro Conservation Area is home to 23,000 Maasai but regulations have restricted their possibilities for livestock-keeping and agriculture as well as access to grazing areas and essential water sources. These same areas have been developed for tourism, with camp-sites, problems of rubbish, track erosion, disturbance to wildlife and the destruction of vegetation and archaeological sites.[48]

RECOMMENDATIONS

The tourism industry should:

• Respect the needs and aspirations of local people.

• Support the concept that local people should determine their own development.

• Actively encourage local community involvement in tourism projects.

• Promote the active partnership of local people and communities in tourism development.

• Involve the widest range of local associations.

• Actively support local enterprises and cooperatives which provide services, goods and crafts.

• Support locally-owned shops, restaurants and guide services.

• Involve local people through employment at all levels.

• Encourage the development of home-based tourism accommodation and facilities.

• Prevent disruption to and the displacement of local people.

CONSULTING STAKEHOLDERS AND THE PUBLIC

Consultation between the tourism industry and local communities, organisations and institutions is essential if they are to work alongside each other and resolve potential conflicts of interest

- Consultation is a process which aims to reconcile economic development with the broader interests of local people and the potential impact of development on their natural, social and cultural environment. Consultation between government, industry and local people is essential in order to assess a development project, ways of minimising its negative impacts and of maximising local people's positive contribution.

- Projects which are imposed from 'outside' or 'above' often fail to take account of local natural and human resources and interests. Lack of consultation between public and private bodies and local communities may cause hostility and opposition and make it even harder to resolve conflicts of interest.

- Local communities worldwide are at the forefront of environmental conservation, having the best first-hand knowledge and the most interest in protecting their own environment.

- Sustainable development means taking account of people's present and future needs and welfare based on their informed choice and understanding of the environmental, social and cultural costs of development. Consultation is central to this since it means exchanging information and opinion, evaluation and action, based on local expertise, knowledge and resources.

Tourism and consultation

- Lack of consultation in tourism has often resulted in accelerated hardships for local people, especially in developing countries. These include increased land prices, urbanisation and acculturation, damage to natural resources, the uprooting of whole villages and the abandonment of traditional occupations such as agriculture, herding and fishing. This has been the case from Austria to Spain and Switzerland – from the Dominican Republic to Gambia, India, Kenya, Sri Lanka and Thailand.

- Growing concern at the economic, environmental, social and cultural impacts of tourism illustrates the need for improved levels of consultation in tourism decision-making. Actions taken without regard to local needs and wishes and without consultation have resulted in the opposition of local people, non-governmental organisations and academics, and the formation of protest groups in such places as Goa and Thailand.

In Hawaii, community opposition to tourism development has usually been based on cultural issues. A 1989 conference on the impact of tourism declared: "Contrary to the claims of its promoters, tourism... has not benefited the poor and oppressed native Hawaiian people. Tourism is not an indigenous practice, nor has it been initiated by the native Hawaiian people... Its primary purpose is to make money. As such tourism is a new form of exploitation... which perpetuates poverty... sexism and racism... (and) is detrimental to the life, well-being and spiritual health of native Hawaiian people... All is not well in 'paradise'."[49]

- The need for consultation across a broad spectrum to benefit both local communities, tourists and the industry, is being recognised in some areas. In Wales the Festival of the Countryside is directed by a non-governmental organisation – CYNEFIN – which works closely with the Development Board for Rural Wales, the Countryside Council for Wales, the Wales Tourist Board, local authorities and others. In Dorset the Brit Valley Tourism Development Forum aims to respond to community concerns and aspirations, and involves the community in Tourism Action Teams.

- However, business enterprises do continue to implement projects without consulting local communities, often with the cooperation of local or national authorities and even where consultation is advocated. Thus, while the Malaysian Town and Country Planning Act calls for structural planning for tourism developments and for EIAs the authorities have brushed aside local protests on the basis that "we don't have to consult local people since we know what's good for them[50]...". Overriding or ignoring local sentiments cannot be in the industry's interests.

- Tourism brings local people into direct contact with tourists whose cultural practices and religious beliefs are different from their own. Recognising the universal right of people to privacy and to conduct their lives in accordance with their own traditions and customs, consultation provides local communities with a greater say in the scale, pace and nature of contact with tourists and improves relations between the industry, guests and hosts.

- The impact of mass tourism poses a serious threat to such traditions as hospitality to strangers, which is still considered an obligation by many peoples like the Bedouin and Tuareg whose nomadic lifestyles have been restricted and whose encampments are periodically raided by tea-drinking tourist hordes.

Tourism is one of Jordan's major sources of foreign currency. The Bedouin of Petra used to offer traditional hospitality to all visitors. Being members of a poor tribe, they experience hardships as a result of feeding extra mouths. It was expected that visitors would leave a gift, no matter how small, for their hosts. But tourist abuse of Bedouin hospitality has changed this – although hospitality is still offered, the Bedouin now expect to be paid in cash.[51] Consultation could help such traditions to be maintained.

- The process of consultation is essential in order to inform local residents of the economic implications of changes brought about by the rapid growth of tourism and its associated risks, and of the potential benefits of appropriate or sustainable tourism.

- Local people have a greater long-term stake in and commitment to environmental protection than national and international organisations who relocate when environmental degradation leads to diminishing returns. Local people generally have no such choice.

The Eco Institute of Costa Rica, a non-profit organisation headed by Maurice Strong, has created a think-tank for tourism in Central America. It brings together government officials, private developers, community activists, environmentalists and the tourism industry to exchange ideas for constructive and sustainable tourism planning. The institute aims to influence government policies, represent community and conservation interests, coordinate appropriate development projects and mitigate the negative impacts of

tourism (such as the over-use of resources, crime, rising prices, prostitution, over-development, pollution, vanishing wildlife, crowded beaches, social inequality). The institute aims to change the tourism profile of Central America by providing a viable model for other countries in the region that are turning to tourism, involving marginal groups and making tourism a sustainable form of development.[52]

RECOMMENDATIONS

The tourism industry should:

• Consult with and inform local residents about potential changes induced by the rapid growth of tourism.

• Consult with and inform local residents of the potential benefits of non–intrusive, sustainable tourism.

• Introduce measures at the planning stage to encourage greater local consultation.

• Hold workshops, meetings and other public fora for consultation.

• Support the establishment of proper mechanisms for efficient local consultation.

• Consult with the widest variety of local associations, including non-governmental organisations, in order to integrate public and private interests.

• Fully inform and consult with local government and non-government bodies prior to and during the implementation of tourism projects.

TRAINING STAFF

Staff training which integrates sustainable tourism into work practices, along with recruitment of local personnel at all levels, improves the quality of the tourism product

- A skilled and trained workforce not only benefits an industry economically but improves the quality of a product, efficiency at all levels and the confidence, self-esteem and commitment of employees.

- In Europe the importance of integrating environmental training into all elements of policy-making is gaining ground. An EC project has been set up to further environmental studies in schools, promote training schemes for professionals, and hold regular conferences and seminars on all aspects of environmental protection.[53]

- Sustainable development emphasises the need for improved education in order to promote social and economic well-being. Education and training in environmental awareness and management, essential for integrated and sustainable development, must include social and cultural as well as economic issues.

Training in tourism

- Incorporating environmental awareness and management into training in the tourism industry would be a step towards ensuring the implementation of environmental policies and legislation in tourism enterprises.

- Although tourism is the world's largest industry, jobs in the industry generally have a low status. Proper training and increased staff and student awareness of the importance and complexity of tourism within a broad social, economic and environmental context, would help foster pride in the job and destination and in turn improve the tourism product for consumers, hosts and the industry.

- Staff such as booking clerks, tour leaders and guides, who are on the 'front line' of tourism, are often better placed than office-bound company directors or managers to witness its environmental, social and practical impacts. Their opinions and experience, particularly if they are properly trained, can provide a valuable service to the industry, host communities and tourists alike.

- Properly trained staff can encourage a sense of responsibility and environmental awareness in tourists which, in turn, will lead to a longer-term and more sustainable industry.

• Many conservation schemes, supported by tourism revenue, are directed by expatriate 'experts' who often lack first-hand familiarity with local conditions and needs. The training of local people to manage their own projects can avoid misunderstanding and possible hostility.

On wildlife reserves, such as the elephant conservation projects in Zambia, the training of local people as guards and tourist and hunting safari guides, has not only provided stable jobs and incomes to people, some of whom were previously poachers, but has raised the quality of safari tours.

• Training should include multi-cultural education that aims to foster an understanding and appreciation of cultural differences and to make tourism staff and students aware of the needs and expectations of both 'guests' and 'hosts'. It could also help to eliminate prejudice and xenophobia. Cultural interchange programmes, reinforced by good practice, may further contribute to removing the stigma attached to tourism in some destinations as a form of colonialism.

• Proper training can nurture a caring attitude towards a country, its people, culture, traditions, religion and way of life.

The St Lucia Rainforest Tours Project channels its profits back into educational programmes. These include a monthly schools broadsheet, field trips for school children and regular lectures from the Forestry Department staff, leading to an appreciation of the value of the forest among St Lucians as well as tourists.[54]

• Where the local workforce is untrained it may be expedient in the short-term to import trained labour. However, longer term advantages for all entail training and employing staff from the local community. This applies particularly to tour leaders or guides who have an intimate knowledge of and vested interest in the area and whose involvement will improve the quality of service.

• Tourism is often advocated as a means of raising educational levels in developing countries. Although there is scope for training in catering, hotel management, tourism promotion, sales and marketing, in practice most of these roles are filled by expatriate personnel.[55] Training

of local personnel must not be restricted to low paid and low status jobs.

• Training can be at home or abroad, ranging from in-house short courses to longer college-based programmes, according to requirement. Local training may prove more cost-effective for both the industry and the national or local authorities, as well as promoting and making better use of local skills, handicrafts and produce.

The Kenyan hotel chain, African Tours and Hotels, provides management services for other hotels, while Kenya's Utalii College provides training for the country's own nationals as well as those of other African countries.[56]

• The provision of training by private investors in tourism, often with the possibility of sending staff overseas, can relieve host governments of the cost of training, particularly in developing countries.[57] On the other hand, the advantage of local training is in decreasing payments abroad for training and the ability to reflect local characteristics and specific needs.

RECOMMENDATIONS

The tourism industry should:

- Integrate environmental, social and cultural issues into training programmes.

- Enhance the status of local staff at all levels as an essential part of the industry.

- Foster a sense of pride in the job and care for the destination and its people.

- Train staff in understanding the complex nature of modern tourism.

- Explore the positive and negative impacts of tourism on host communities, during training.

- Train staff to foster tourist responsibility towards the destination country.

- Encourage multi-cultural education and interchange programmes.

- Train local staff for managerial and leadership positions.

- Channel back profits from tourism into educational programmes which encourage an appreciation of the environment and heritage.

MARKETING TOURISM RESPONSIBLY

Marketing that provides tourists with full and responsible information increases respect for the natural, social and cultural environments of destination areas and enhances customer satisfaction

- Marketing and advertising are powerful forces in the successful selling of any product. In a predominantly consumer society, competitive marketing is based on respecting people's preferences.

- Consumer protection legislation in many countries rules that marketing and advertising must not make misleading claims about products. European consumer policy stresses consumers' rights to protection of health, safety and economic interests, and rights of representation, redress, information and education in order to make informed choices on the market.

- Sustainable development rests on full and honest marketing that provides information about products and the companies which produce them, including their impact on employees and the environment. Such marketing aims to improve the quality of natural and human-made environments and living standards and takes into account the cost of environmental assets. It considers the needs of future as well as present generations.

Marketing tourism

- The principles of sustainability apply to the whole industry, especially the mass market. They are not limited to 'alternative' or 'green' holidays, and, above all, must not be simply a marketing ploy. The Inter-Continental Hotel group policy statement warns of "…the negative publicity being received by companies which make superficial changes to their products and market them as 'environmentally friendly' despite the products remaining harmful in reality."

- Marketing strategy for sustainable tourism involves identifying, appraising and constantly reviewing both the supply of natural, social, cultural and other resources, as well as the demand side.

- With the growth of tourism and the interchangeability of holiday destinations, tourism marketing is especially competitive. It is unique since the consumer buys the product 'blind' – the holiday destination cannot be inspected or tested before it is bought – since it is the consumer who goes to the product and 'consumes' it at source, rather than vice-versa.

- The success of a particular destination depends on marketing which is predominantly controlled by tour operators in tourist-generating countries, who have the power to 'make or break' a destination and who thus have a particular responsibility towards those countries dependent on tourism for foreign currency.

- Tourist marketing is pre-eminently about selling dreams. Tourists' impressions and expectations are generally formed before they reach a destination, through the promotional material and support services of international companies, travel agents, tour operators, airlines, national tourist boards. Brochures, travel articles, guidebooks and television documentaries all have immense power to influence tourists' attitudes and behaviour.

- Full and responsible marketing of tourism destinations can raise awareness, appreciation and respect for local culture and environment, and can also increase overall customer satisfaction. For example, the Ceilidh Place in Ullapool introduces visitors to the Scottish Highland tradition of the Ceilidh, while providing local musicians and storytellers with an opportunity to practice their arts.

The Kuloro 'Wildlife in the Gambia' project encourages conservation projects alongside traditional farming techniques. Tourists are informed they will be staying in simple accommodation with basic facilities and are advised on appropriate dress, local words of greeting and the cultural background of the area.[58]

- Unreal expectations created by inaccurate or insufficient information give rise to misunderstanding and disappointment on the part of tourists, which may then lead to criticism and intolerance of host communities, and sometimes of the whole tourism product. Honest marketing can help prevent such scenarios. A European Commission directive on package tours[59] stipulates that brochures "may not make misleading claims, but must provide clear and precise information…" on such practical aspects as price, transport, accommodation and visa requirements. Following this directive is clearly beneficial to the industry, their customers and the destination countries.

- Host communities and countries are also affected by negative marketing which perpetuates stereotypes of peoples, cultures and environments and reduces them to a few instantly recognisable characteristics. The industry has both a moral responsibility and practical interest in preventing such negative marketing.

In Hawaii, 'Hula marketing' for the express purpose of economic benefit, romanticises Hawaiian culture to appeal to tourists' exotic fantasies. Typical images are smiling, flower-adorned girls, hula dancers and moonlight feasts served by obliging natives. Such marketing perpetuates racist and sexist stereotypes and promotes a cultural image that disregards the real lives of native Hawaiians struggling to survive. Meanwhile, the Hawaiian state government gives financial support to the Hawaii Visitors Bureau, while the authentic and living Hawaiian culture and language of local communities is neglected.[60]

- Tour guides employed by the industry in destination areas facilitate contact between hosts and guests. They, therefore, have an obligation to provide honest information and to encourage tourists to behave respectfully.

- Ostentatious displays of wealth, conspicuous consumption and inappropriate styles of dress and conduct can provoke negative responses. Traditional values may be undermined by the open consumption of alcohol in cultures where it is forbidden or discouraged and may well lead to resentment. It is in the industry's interest to inform tourists about a destination in order to lessen negative responses, increase respect for the host culture and environment and prevent disappointment and misunderstanding. Initiatives such as that taken by British Airways,[61] which includes greater information to customers on the impact of tourism on destinations, are to be welcomed.

RECOMMENDATIONS

The tourism industry should:

• Ensure that the marketing of 'green' tourism is not merely a selling ploy but reflects sound environmental policy and practice.

• Educate visitors in advance of arrival and give guidance on environmental 'dos' as well as 'don'ts'.

• Dismantle racial, sexual, cultural or religious stereotyping within the industry.

• Use marketing strategies that respect the peoples, communities and environments of destination areas, and which are non-exploitative.

• Make tourists aware of their potential impact on and their responsibilities towards host societies.

• Provide tourists with full and fair information that enables them to understand all environmental and related aspects of holidays when selecting any destination or holiday package.

• Market holidays that correspond to the tourist product and experience offered.

• Provide information to tourists on respecting the cultural and natural heritage of destination areas.

• Not impose western mores on countries with different values; e.g. bathing topless.

• Encourage tourists to try new experiences, such as cuisines, cultures and ways of life.

• Promote tourism appropriate to the capacities of a destination in terms of the scale, numbers and types of tourist.

• Not encourage tourism to vulnerable ethnic groups or environments.

• Employ tour guides who attempt to portray societies honestly and dispel stereotypes.

• Provide customers with detailed pre-departure information which can be reinforced in flight and which may include:
 – A reminder that they are 'guests' and should act accordingly by not imposing their own standards and attitudes on their 'hosts'.
 – Conversational phrases in the local language rather than simply demands.
 – Advice on acceptable behaviour, including dress, information on religious customs, food, drink, transport, history and politics.

UNDERTAKING RESEARCH

On-going research and monitoring by the industry using effective data collection and analysis is essential to help solve problems and to bring benefits to destinations, the industry and consumers

- Pre-project planning and research usually concentrate on economic feasibility and fail to take 'invisible' environmental or social costs into account. Even when feasibility prior to establishing a project or enterprise may be assessed, the on-going progress and wider impacts of development are rarely monitored. In addition, such research that is carried out appears to be directed towards problem-solving rather than problem-avoiding.

- Research information and data are not usually available to the general public nor, more importantly, to those most directly affected by a project.

Tourism and research

- For the tourism industry to develop and survive in a sustainable and responsible manner an anticipatory approach is essential. Anticipating problems and absorbing the costs of problem-solving in advance may mean short-term costs but in the long run is likely to be cheaper.

- Where tourism has damaged the environment, such as in the Mediterranean Costas, better anticipatory research, education and implementation could have avoided or reduced problems. This also applies to such areas as the Lake District, the Alps, numerous tropical islands and game reserves.

- A reactive approach of delaying problem-solving may be acceptable only if it is accompanied by research into generating better information and cheaper, more effective solutions, and is not simply aimed at postponing action and costs.

- The rapid pace of tourism development in economically, socially and environmentally vulnerable areas, which are often characterised by a paucity of data and by data-gathering difficulties, shows the urgent need for more basic research.

One form of research that could usefully be adopted to the field of tourism development is Rapid Rural Appraisal (RRA), which originated in the field of rural development. RRA adopts the perspective of local people on economic, social and environmental issues. Its flexible technique, using local expertise, semi-structured questionnaires, observation, diagrams and photographs, aims at making rapid assessments of local conditions. RRA can also be adopted to urban environments and can be used in both developing and developed countries and areas.[62]

• Proper research, which addresses the central problem of how to assess the social, cultural and environmental impacts of tourism, is advantageous to the tourism industry as a whole. Some of the problems which such research should consider are the impact of tourism within the context of other processes of development, modernisation and trade. The considerable time-lag between the expansion of tourism and the onset of negative effects, and the opinion, evaluation and participation of local people in assessing the impacts of tourism on their society and culture must also be taken into consideration.

• Proper pre-project research must examine who the tourists to a particular destination are, why they travel, what their images and expectations are, and what factors govern their behaviour and attitudes towards their 'hosts'. Without such an understanding, it is virtually impossible to broker more sustainable forms of tourism. Appropriate tourists in appropriate destinations are more likely to ensure longer-term viability.

• The tourism industry, together with academic institutions, non-governmental organisations, governments, planners and the public are increasingly aware of the importance of tourism. Although research into its effects is gaining credibility, much information originates from secondary sources. More primary research in both tourism-generating and receiving countries is essential in order to improve knowledge and understanding, and to test models and hypotheses for sustainable tourism.

• A growing volume of data is being collected by national tourism agencies, international tour operators and bodies such as the United Nations and the World Tourism Organisation. However, motives, criteria, survey efficiency, data processing, comparability and the dissemination of results remain problematic and call for continued research.

The Lake District National Park is developing a computerised survey of its landscape using a Geographic Information System (GIS) to monitor both the natural environment and human habitation. The system can also provide information of relevance to tourism, such as footpath erosion.[63]

• Thorough research requires real partnerships in money, skills and organisational resources which, in turn, entails political will, honesty and professional commitment. Figures can be fudged, conferences stage-managed, plans cosmeticised, research ill-funded and criticism conveniently silenced. Everyone, including the manipulating powerful interests, loses out in the end.

• Research and campaigning bodies, such as the Ecumenical Coalition on Third World Tourism (ECTWT) in Thailand, Equations in India, and pressure groups like Tourism Concern are crucial for the growth of just, participatory and sustainable tourism development. The industry can benefit from such expertise.

RECOMMENDATIONS

The tourism industry should:

- Initiate, encourage and support research into prior assessment and monitoring techniques for measurement of environmental, social and economic impacts, particularly in areas or countries which currently lack adequate resources for this.

- Carry out research into improving Environmental Impact Assessments (EIAs) and other project assessment techniques in relation to tourism.

- Conduct and support research into methods for anticipating the impacts of tourism, as well as reactive problem-solving techniques.

- Improve valuation techniques to ensure that analyses include wider environmental and social aspects.

- Ensure that the results of research and any relevant information are disseminated to the institutions and individuals responsible for tourism decision-making.

- Make the results of research and studies available to local and national authorities, tourism staff and to the general public.

- Carry out studies using local expertise, experience and opinions.

ANNAPURNA CONSERVATION AREA PROJECT, NEPAL

Dr Chandra Prasad Gurung

Project Director

Annapurna Conservation Area Project (ACAP)

Katmandu, Nepal

The project area

Surrounded by some of the highest mountains on earth and bisected by equally deep valleys, the Annapurna region in Nepal is a land of extremes. More than 40,000 people of various ethnic and religious backgrounds have inhabited the region for centuries. Due to various climatic conditions, from sub-tropical to temperate and arid and desert types, the area is endowed with excellent habitats for various flora and fauna; the endangered snow leopard, blue sheep, more than 100 varieties of orchids and some of the largest rhododendron forests in the world. Most of the inhabitants are subsistence farmers, surviving on the natural resources of the area and developing their own traditional management systems.

The problems

Trekking tourism, which has had a phenomenal increase during the past two decades, has upset this delicate ecological balance between land and life in the Himalaya. The demands of the tourists far exceed what the area can provide, compounding the pre-existing problems of a growing local population. The Annapurna's natural resources have been stretched to their limit and the area is on the verge of crisis.

1 Each year, over 36,000 trekkers and 36,000 porters visit the Annapurna region which supports 40,000 local inhabitants. These local residents are mostly subsistence farmers.

2 About 60 per cent of these trekkers come during four months of the year (October–November and March–April). They are concentrated in few places, resulting in devastating impacts on both local cultural and natural environments.

3 86 per cent of Nepal's energy comes from forests. Current figures show that these forests are disappearing at a rate of three per cent per year. In the Annapurna virtually everybody depends on fuelwood for cooking as there are no alternative sources of energy.

4 The lodges in one small village along the major Annapurna trekking route consume one hectare of

virgin rhododendron forest per year to service the needs of trekkers. There are 850 lodges throughout the Annapurna region.

5   One hectare of cleared forests loses 30-75 tons of soil annually. In Nepal, approximately 400,000 hectares are cleared each year, resulting in devastating landslides and floods.

6   Tourism, which is one of the main sources of foreign exchange income for Nepal, is deceiving for local people. In the Annapurna, only twenty cents out of the three dollars spent by an average trekker per day contributes to local village economies. The rest is spent on imported goods and services from the towns especially from Pokhara, Katmandu or the trekker's home countries.

ACAP: an integrated approach

Increasing concern for the negative impacts of tourism on the natural environment, village economies and cultural traditions resulted in the establishment of the Annapurna Conservation Area Project (ACAP) in December 1986, headquartered at Ghandruk village en route to the Annapurna Sanctuary. The project covers approximately 2,600 sq km. ACAP addresses three main aspects simultaneously: nature conservation, human development and tourism management. The main focus of the project is the people and not flora and fauna. The conservation area practices multiple land use methods of resource management to combine environmental protection with sustainable community development. All the activities are carried out on the basis of three principles: sustainability, people's participation and ACAP's catalytic role.

ACAP strives to ensure that the beneficiaries from trekking tourism and conservation activities will be the local people, at the same time making them the guardians of their resources. The approach is that of a grassroots philosophy that strongly discourages a handout philosophy. As a result traditional subsistence activities are woven into a framework of sound resource management, supplemented by small scale conservation and alternative energy projects

to minimise impact of tourists and upgrade the local standard of living.

ACAP has been implemented by the King Mahendra Trust for Nature Conservation (KMTNC). KMTNC is a non-governmental, autonomous, non-profit organisation dedicated for the promotion and conservation of natural and cultural heritage of Nepal.

Objectives of the project

The main objectives of the project are to protect the natural and cultural environments of the Annapurna region for the benefit of its 40,000 inhabitants, as well as for the international visitors, while raising their awareness about the fragility of the environment.

Work undertaken

ACAP's activities fall into eight categories:

1   Forest Conservation

2   Alternative Energy

3   Conservation Education

4   Tourism Management

5   Community Development

6   Community Health and Sanitation

7   Community Management Committees

8   Research and Training

Tourism management

In order to reduce the impacts of trekking tourism as well as to make the tourism sustainable the following activities have been initiated:

Lodge owner training

Most of the lodge owners in the Annapurna area are illiterate and have changed their occupation from sheep-herding.

They only knew about using firewood to provide warmth for the trekkers, providing hot water even in the most remote areas and using local timbers and bamboos for the construction of lodges. In some cases, the safety of the trekkers was questionable.

In conjunction with the Hotel Management Tourism and Training Centre (HMTTC), ACAP developed an integrated curriculum where food preparation, sanitation, garbage disposal, menu costing, low cost, appropriate fuelwood-saving devices and safety and security of the trekkers were included. A week long training course has been provided at various places in the Annapurna region. At the end of the training, lodge management committees have been formed. Now, the hotels at Chhomrong and all the lodges in the sanctuary are much safer and cleaner and have installed fuelwood saving technologies, such as back-boiler water heaters and solar water heaters.

Litter and pollution control

Many famous trekking trails are known as "toilet paper trails". Even in the largest lodges in Annapurna toilets virtually did not exist. Empty beer bottles, water bottles and cans also caused problems.

Initially, ACAP created a revolving fund to provide loans to the lodge owners for toilet construction. The loans have been a very big incentive. All the lodges now have toilets and have built garbage pits.

ACAP has launched cleaning campaigns bringing together local people, students from local schools and ACAP staff. This has been very effective in raising awareness about environmental conservation.

ACAP has also developed a "minimum impact code" and a brochure distributed to all trekkers going into the Annapurna region. This provides basic information to the trekkers so that they can be well prepared prior to their departure. Furthermore, ACAP has established "visitor information centres" at various places where necessary information including videos are shown to the trekkers.

Ecotourism development

ACAP now plans to develop two "Ecotourist areas". One would be nature orientated, the other would encompass a mixture of nature and cultural activities. Lodges will be placed at appropriate distances rather than spreading everywhere, allowing a controlled number of trekkers into the two areas. It is hoped that the trekkers will feel that they have been contributing to the protection of natural and cultural environments, as well as feeling safer and happier while trekking in these areas. Ultimately, ACAP hopes that these two areas will become a model for a sustainable tourism management not only in ACAP but also in Nepal.

Conclusion

After working for over five years, many improvements in the protection of the natural and cultural environments can be seen in the Annapurna areas:

- Lodges are cleaner and more pleasant.
- Less firewood is being used as solar water heaters and back-boiler water heaters are employed for hot water.
- Food preparation has improved.
- Kerosene-only policies have been enforced in certain key areas.
- Hunting has been completely banned.
- Income generating training provided to the local people, such as poultry raising, carpet weaving and vegetable farming, means that more money has been retained in the villages.
- As the lodges have become cleaner and more hygienic, the tourists are not afraid to stay in them, thus generating more income and employment opportunities for the local people.

ACAP feels that its efforts are proving successful in protecting the natural and traditional local environments, as well as bringing the local people into the mainstream of conservation activity where they feel that the resources belong to them and that they must act to protect them.

ANNAPURNA CONSERVATION AREA PROJECT • NEPAL

INTEGRATED RURAL TOURISM
LOWER CASAMANCE, SENEGAL

Amadou Mactar Gningue

Coordinateur de Tourisme

Senegalese Embassy, London

in association with Raoul Bianchi

Traditional forms of tourism development in Africa provide the tourist with the illusion of risk and adventure from a strong base of familiarity and the minimum of socio-cultural interaction. The high levels of foreign capital participation ensures that the operation and management of the industry remains largely in the hands of foreign multinationals and members of the indigenous business elite.

Tourism has played a significant role in Senegal's economic development. There has been considerable growth of large scale developments reliant on foreign capital and management along the coastline, particularly around Dakar, Saly Portudal and in the south at Cap Skirring. Characteristically the development of coastal hotels and resorts has been relatively unplanned. Mostly they provide only service and unskilled employment for the local population. There is a also a high degree of social and physical segregation emphasised by walls and the presence of guards intended to keep locals out of these tourist areas. The entire structure of the tourist system undermines any possibility of a meaningful social exchange between tourists and hosts.

'Tourism for Discovery'

In 1971 the government of Senegal with the help of an international organisation of French-speaking countries, l'Agence de Cooperation Culturelle et Technique (ACCT), under the guidance of a French anthropologist, Christian Saglio, drew up plans for an innovative tourism development project designed specifically to ensure local involvement at every level and maximum benefits for the community.

The Lower Casamance, a lush and fertile region between The Gambia and the southern border of Senegal, was chosen as the location of the 'Tourism for Discovery' project. The area is largely inhabited by the Diola tribe in traditional villages. Of exceptional ecological importance, as well as rich in tradition and folklore, the Casamance provided an ideal location for an experimental project which would attempt to exploit the area's unique tourism attraction, whilst preserving its socio-cultural and environmental integrity.

The project set out primarily to integrate tourism gradually into the indigenous society and foster a type of tourism whereby host-tourist relationships are more 'personalised' and the visitor is treated as a guest rather than an intruder. The scheme also sought to emphasise the role of the community in its development and ensure that it secured the maximum benefits from tourism.

The 'Tourism for Discovery' project revolves around a model based on accommodating a controlled number of tourists in simple lodgings built, managed and operated by the local villagers. Using traditional materials (wood, mud and palm-thatch) the lodgings or 'campements villageois' have been built close to established local villages in accordance with local architectural styles minimising any contrasts between the tourist facilities and local living conditions. All the campements are equipped with basic sanitation, running water and kerosene lamps for lighting.

Access to the campements is via local transport (bush taxis and canoes) and natural communication routes, particularly the intricate network of waterways. Not only does this limit any potential destruction caused by the installation of more conventional modes of transport but it also provides the tourist with a genuine sensation of discovery and immersion in the local environment. Meals are prepared using traditional recipes and locally grown produce wherever possible. Activities focus on nature excursions, local village life and informal talks by villagers on the history and culture of the area. Social interaction is extensive and many visitors even assist locals in day-to-day agricultural and construction projects.

Implementation of the Scheme

The 'Tourism for Discovery' project began in 1972. An initial investment of FCFA 2 million ($7,000 app.) per camp, to cover construction costs, was provided by the ACCT for the first four pilot campements at Elinkine, Enampore, Tionk-Essil and Baila. The first campement began operation in November 1973 at Elinkine, closely followed by Enampore in January 1974 and the remaining two in January 1976. During its first full year of operation Enampore generated profits of FCFA 1.2 million ($4,000 app.).

Implementation of the project was not without difficulty, not least the problem of introducing a monetary system of exchange into a local economy based primarily on subsistence. Accustomed to the large-scale projects more often associated with tourism, the local communities were initially suspicious of the project, fearing social upheaval in their villages and doubting the desire of tourists to adapt to rural African life. Nevertheless after a long series of public consultations and numerous meetings among traditional chiefs and village leaders disagreements were resolved and the local people convinced of the project's viability. The consultations and discussions were part of a lengthy educational process vital to the success of the project and were in-keeping with the respect for democracy prevalent in traditional African societies.

By 1983 a further five campements had been built, in Koubalan, Affiniam and Abene with the aid of the Canadian University Service Overseas (CUSO), and in Oussouye and Sine Saloum, financed by the French government. With a combined capacity of 310 bed spaces, 13,000 bed nights per year were being recorded.

Oussouye

Oussouye was the ninth campement to be built in the Casamance, with an initial outlay of FCFA 3 million ($10,000 app.) provided by the French government aid scheme 'Fonds d'Aide et de Cooperation' (FAC). During the first period of operation from December 1982 to February 1983, the campement generated FCFA 1.3 million ($5,000 app.) in profits, which illustrates the rapid return on investment. Leakages are negligible, as the majority of food and supplies are produced locally; the import content ranges from less than five per cent to 50 per cent for products such as sugar. Agriculture is still the chief occupation locally, although the campement has served to boost economic activity in all sectors of the local economy. Similarly the profits generated by tourism have given new life to market gardening and enabled the creation of a furniture workshop, in addition to enhancing essential health and educational facilities.

Stimulated by the modest capital outlay required and the rapid turnover of revenue, small-scale regional promoters are duplicating the village models of the Casamance and building similar tourist centres outside the region. By the end of the decade the 13 operational campements (total capacity 500 bed spaces) were playing host to nearly 20,000 visitors per year, bringing in a total of FCFA 76 million in revenues (approximately $250,000).

A large part of the scheme's success is due to the capacity of each campement being restricted to a maximum of 20-40 guests at any one time. Similarly the campements are only located in villages of populations of 1,000 inhabitants or more. Pressure to expand is solved by the construction of new campements in other locations rather than the expansion of existing ones. The rationale behind such restrictive measures is to reduce the ratio of visitors to hosts and thereby the risk of saturation and adverse socio-cultural impacts. These could disrupt the delicate social fabric of village life.

Cooperative management

Management and operation of the campements is entirely in the hands of the villagers themselves. Each campement is run as a cooperative with an elected council comprised of village leaders responsible for the allocation and distribution of the revenue at the end of each year. The actual day-to-day operation of each campement is carried out by three small units of two persons, each in charge of a separate function, meals, accommodation and excursions, supervised by a management committee. Prices and remuneration for each worker are also agreed communally.

This cooperative campement system has generated substantial economic activity within participating villages, and its strong emphasis on local participation has ensured that a predominant share of the revenue accrued from tourism remains in the villages and is used to improve the villagers quality of life. Priority is reserved for improving community facilities, particularly health and educational facilities. The cooperative in Elinkine has financed a maternity clinic and a school extension entirely from the profits generated by tourism. Profits have also been used to

finance other activities ranging from vegetable farming (the market garden in Oussouye), raising livestock, fishing (the Elinkine cooperative has also bought a canoe and outboard motor) and crafts such as the furniture workshop created in Oussouye. Apart from the overall supervision of the project by a regional coordinator in the regional capital of Ziguinchor, the government does not levy taxes on the campements and has thereby delegated the responsibility of public expenditure down to the village cooperatives. Furthermore, the project has provided substantial employment for the young (approximately half the population of Oussouye are under 20 years old) and discouraged them from migrating to the larger towns in search of employment – a serious problem throughout the developing world.

Tourism for Discovery – A model for the future?

The village-based campement model represents a departure from traditional forms of tourism development and represents a progressive attempt to generate sustainable economic activity without disrupting the social, cultural and environmental integrity of the community on which it depends. The low investment costs, modest prices and almost immediate returns to the community are three factors integral to the success of the entire project.

Underpinning the success of the campement system is that the villagers themselves know that they are benefiting from the project and the tourists know that their money doesn't leave the villages.

The Casamance experiment is a valuable development model based on prudence and respect for tradition. However, it is still only an isolated project and doubts have even been expressed as to whether it could have survived without the prior growth in mass tourism, with its market and infrastructural support and outside financial assistance. Without addressing the fundamental issues at the heart of the debate for more sustainable tourism, low impact developments such as this will continue to be an 'alternative' to mass tourism rather than the norm, paying lip-service to the need for more radical change in the approach to tourism development. For the time being, however, this is certainly a step in the right direction.

DEVELOPMENT AND THE ENVIRONMENT CENTER PARCS

Clive Gordon

The Environment & Development Company Ltd
Nottingham, UK

Introduction

Center Parcs is the Dutch holiday village company which, in the 1980s, had a significant influence on the development of the holiday village/holiday centre market in Europe. In particular, it has influenced attitudes towards all-year-round operation, the short-break market and environmental practice.

Company history

In 1968 the company bought the land and opened the first small holiday village in the Limburg area of The Netherlands. The 60 villas set in woodlands and grouped around a canvas covered swimming pool were the genesis of the villages as they are now designed.

Early success encouraged further growth and the development of new sites through the 1970s. Concern for the countryside and trees formed the basis of an early commitment to landscape enhancement.

Today there are 13 villages flourishing with year-round occupancy levels of 90-95 per cent in The Netherlands, Belgium, France and the U.K. There are plans for additional villages in France, Belgium and the UK.

In 1983 Piet Derksen, the owner and founder of Sporthuis Centrum, transferred most of the shares in the company to the Christian 'Living Waters Foundation' which he established to aid work in developing countries and among disadvantaged peoples. 25 per cent of the company's shares were launched on the Dutch stock market in 1985, achieving an over subscription of forty-to-one and a doubling of the share value within a year.

1989 saw the takeover of the Company by Scottish and Newcastle Breweries and the retirement of Piet Derksen at the age of 75. The investment has proved very worthwhile for Scottish and Newcastle, making a significant contribution to the Company's profits in 1991.

The product

The Center Parcs Holiday Village concept is a blend of self-catering accommodation in the form of villas, backed by a range of sporting and other activities. Their forest setting creates a closeness to nature which enhances their appeal.

The accommodation takes the form of 600-700 single storey holiday villas linked in small groups of two to ten. The groups are designed to ensure the maximum degree of privacy with patios overlooking forest areas and in many of the villages, streams and lakes.

In each of the villages there is a range of central facilities designed to meet the needs of all the guests: indoor and outdoor sports provision, health and beauty facilities and shops, restaurants and bars.

A sub-tropical swimming pool ensures the year-round market for the Center Parcs product. A 5,000 square-metre dome or pyramid filled with subtropical vegetation and a carefully selected range of bathing activities provides for visitor enjoyment.

Environmental and landscape planning and design

In spite of the similarity in the product throughout all the villages, each place has its own unique attributes which depend on the size of the site, its topography, the type of vegetation, its location and the previous uses of the land. The oak woods setting and chateau in the grounds of Le Bois Franc in France, the pine woods, streams and woodland of Sherwood Forest in England, the De Vossemeren lakes in Belgium and the small scale of De Berkenhorst set in the midst of nature reserves in the north of The Netherlands, emphasise the varying nature of each site.

At the root of the company's reputation in the UK is its commitment to the environment, which has led to a handful of major awards and support from organisations such as the Countryside Commission, the English Tourist Board and numerous local authorities.

The aim is to identify sites which not only meet market needs, but also avoid areas of high nature conservation and landscape value. Issues such as traffic generation are not significant for Centre Parcs projects, and are regarded as benign on a development where all cars are returned to

car parks once guests have checked into the villas and where people are expected to walk or cycle during their stay. The choice of conifer plantations, normally uninteresting from an ecological viewpoint, helps to ensure that the development is not seen from outside the Parc. However, it is not sufficient to simply hide a development. If the Company is to make a meaningful long term contribution to the future quality of the environment then it must also enhance the landscape and ecological value of the site.

Sherwood Forest Holiday Village

This was the first Center Parcs development in the UK. A final commitment to proceed with the scheme was made in July 1985 by Center Parcs. Detailed discussions with the local authorities on the economic development, environmental and planning issues had taken place during the previous year. Negotiations involved a wide range of public organisations, government departments and ministers, including the Departments of Employment and Environment, the Nature Conservancy Council, the English Tourist Board and the Forestry Commission – from whom the site was purchased. The company commenced detailed design and submitted planning applications in August 1985. From that moment to the opening of the gates for the first paying guests, the whole development was completed in 21 months. During the same period the company purchased and obtained planning permission at Elveden Forest for its second village in the UK.

Sherwood Forest Holiday Village provides an interesting example of the company's approach to environmental issues. Once the site had been selected, a detailed survey was carried out by an ecologist. This revealed all ecological interest on the site, no matter how small. The subsequent design and layout took into account the findings of the survey which included:

- The careful siting of the villas and central facilities. The blending of the roads and other services into the landscape to ensure a basic layout which respected and built on the attributes of the site.

- The creation of a twelve acre lake and three miles of streams and waterfalls with a rich waterside flora, brought in from a management scheme being carried out at a nearby Site of Special Scientific Interest.
- The subsequent thinning of the existing woodland and opening up of glades to let in light, and the planting of around 500,000 new native trees and bushes.
- The seeding of specially designed grass mixes and wild flowers.
- The creation of a reserve for the special herd of Black Fallow Deer.
- The erection of bird nesting and bat roosting boxes in the conifers helped to ensure the enrichment of the site's wildlife and its value for nature conservation.

The preparation of a detailed management plan which ensured the sensitive development of this initial investment, the opening up and restoration of areas of heathland and a determination to use chemicals only as a last resort, have continued to ensure the long term value of the site. In a period of less than five years since it was completed the site has been recognised for its wildlife including its excellent dragonfly population.

The first two sites did not require formal environmental assessments, but for the most recent development at Longleat in the UK, a comprehensive environmental statement helped to ensure approval of the scheme. The company continuously monitors ecological change with the help of the County Nature Trusts and English Nature.

This investment in the outdoor environment was reinforced indoors by the use of recycled paper for stationery and the installation of collection points to enable the recycling of waste products such as bottles, paper and cans. Energy conservation was also a primary consideration.

Few organisations in the UK were making this level of commitment to the environment in 1985, including those with a remit for environmental management.

Staff commitment

Center Parcs employs some 700 people in each of its UK villages. The essence of the quality of the product and its service lies in the commitment and ability of the staff. The importance placed by the company on its relationship with the outside world and the community in which it operates was also paramount. This commitment was already clearly established through the ownership of the company by a Christian foundation. It was further encouraged in the early stages in the UK through the creation of a 'third world fund', to which all members of staff were invited to contribute 0.25 per cent of their salaries and to manage the scheme. The vast majority responded in a positive way and the fund financed a village development scheme in the Sudan through Action Aid.

Conclusion

There is little doubt that Center Parcs has had a major impact on the development of thinking about sustainable tourism. In particular it has successfully challenged the assumption that all large scale development is bad. However, this does not provide a justification for all large scale schemes. Mass tourism need not be insensitive and badly designed but it demands a different approach, one which seeks harmony with the environment and cultural heritage.

PARTICIPATORY SUSTAINABLE TOURISM FOR GRASSROOTS INCOME GENERATION INDONESIA

Bambang Ismawan

President Director

Bina Swadaya, Jakarta, Indonesia

Background

Uncontrolled tourism has brought negative impacts in Indonesia, ranging from environmental devastation, physical displacement, destruction of traditional lifestyles, to luring women and children into prostitution. Unfortunately, the construction of tourism infrastructure has often sacrificed local farmers as they had to give up their agricultural land without receiving appropriate compensation. Recent examples of this include the displacement incidents at Cimacan Village (West Java) and Wonogiri (Central Java).

Hotels and tourism businesses in the paradise Island of Bali, the main tourist destination in Indonesia, are not controlled or owned by local people but by large investors from Jakarta, in partnership with multinational corporations. Even the Governor of Bali concluded that the increasing revenue from tourism did not affect, or could not be enjoyed, by the majority of the indigenous Balinese people.

The unjust pattern of tourism structure has lead some Indonesian NGOs (Non-Governmental Organisations) and environmental activists to look for alternative solutions. Their aim is to develop the participation of local people, eliminate the burdens placed upon host communities and ensure sustainable tourism activities.

Role of Non-Governmental Organisations

In tourism development NGOs can play a significant role as an intermediary actor between government and profit-orientated private business on one side and the host community's right to sustain its long term aspirations on the other. They can mobilise and strengthen people's organisations and peoples' bargaining power in relation to potential developers. NGOs can also stimulate activity leading to a more equitable sharing of income from tourism.

Bina Swadaya

Bina Swadaya (Community Self-Reliance Development Agency), since its establishment 25 years ago, has been committed to helping raise the standard of living for the rural poor through participation in diversified development efforts.

Driven by concern for the harmful effects of conventional tourism, Bina Swadaya's aim is to generate supplementary income for the host communities, a significant factor in managing sustainable tourism. Bina Swadaya's tourism programme meets the needs of the host community through an equitable distribution of the socio-economic benefits from tourism operations. At the same time it promotes cultural exchange and builds up mutually enriching learning process such as development education, between tourists and hosts.

Project

During the past four years, Bina Swadaya has been offering specific interest tours for open-minded, well-informed, and adventurous travellers both domestic and foreign. The aims of this project are:

1 To introduce the daily life and culture of the host community, as well as showing visitors the development projects in which people are involved in order to increase their socio-economic welfare.

2 To turn tourism activity into a source of supplementary income for the local people. Economic benefit should be equally shared with the host community through using local resources.

3 To encourage cultural exchange in order to promote better understanding of community development programmes in Indonesia.

Feasibility study

As a method in project planning, Bina Swadaya always conduct a feasibility study to identify problems and needs faced by the would-be target groups in the community.

Initiating the idea of a tourism project in 1987, a feasibility study was carried out to collect and gain the optimum information before deciding upon the project's mode of operation. This initial step covered Java and Bali as the pilot project. The six months feasibility study aimed:

1 To identity the impacts of tourism on the local socio-economic base, culture and environment.

2 To assess the needs of people based on their own locally available resources.

3 To carefully study government regulations in the tourism sector in order to set up a suitable model of tourism.

4 To map out the accessibility of local areas and the potential of local products for tourism development.

Finally, the feasibility study recommended an alternative model of tourism which would strengthen the socio-economic capability of the host community.

Planning and implementation

From the recommended feasibility study, specific interest tours were drawn up in the form of alternative tour packages for both the domestic and international market. The content of the tour programme combined study of development projects and leisure travel without neglecting the primary mission and objectives.

In order to minimise misunderstanding and misconceptions, participation by the local people is vital in the first stage of planning an alternative tour programme. Through field worker guidance the host community have to be advised on planning of the tours, especially those including aspects of their daily life and basic social norms which are to be shared with visitors. The tour planning also includes preparing and selecting the host communities. In this stage field workers acting as facilitators play a significant role in communicating the purpose of the tours to the local people. Advance briefing relates to the purpose of the visit, background of visitors, and other practical requirements. This is absolutely necessary in order to smooth the process of interaction, to build up a genuine relationship and to ensure the use of local products for local income generation.

Since its initiation Bina Swadaya's tourism project has organised various group tours interested in development issues and projects. The arrangement is for semi-organised tours. Bina Swadaya acts only as facilitator. Apart from the direct income from services provided to the visitors or by selling local products, the host community receives a small donation from Bina Swadaya. Delivered through local existing organisations (self-help groups or community based cooperatives), the donation is intended to strengthen their financial ability to manage this activity.

PARTICIPATORY SUSTAINABLE TOURISM FOR GRASSROOTS INCOME GENERATION • INDONESIA

Monitoring and evaluation

Monitoring the activity is vital, especially for observing the extent of the tourism impacts upon the target groups. Improvements can thus be made and any problems discussed through the mechanism called 'musyawarah' (consultation to reach consensus).

Monitoring of the tourism projects is regularly reported by Bina Swadaya's field workers, who provide guidance and assistance to the served target groups. The content of the tour programmes are actually integrated and incorporated into the primary development projects managed by Bina Swadaya or other local NGOs. Therefore, visits to development projects or village-stay programmes are additional components of the project and are viewed as a part of the integrated approach.

The tourism management project can be evaluated as:

Socio-economic impact

The absorption of local products, accommodation and food services and handicrafts, obviously brings advantages in terms of increasing supplementary income for the local people and thus economically strengthen local organisations. At the micro economic level, the arrival of visitors encourages the gradual growth of other productive activity and also creates job opportunities.

Psychological and cultural impact

Field experience proves that this pattern of participatory tourism may slowly increase the level of participation by local people in development activities. The recognition of people's efforts boosts self-pride and self-reliance. Culturally, it preserves and revives traditional products, art and culture which are to some extent disappearing.

Environmental impact

This impact is clearly seen in the social forestry project managed by Bina Swadaya. Visits to the forest farmer groups is seen as an instrument which increases awareness and the sense of belonging toward the forest which eventually leads to environmental preservation activities. The people living in the area of forest are directly involved in the forest management.

Conclusion

The tourism industry as a part of primary development activity has inevitably become a growing phenomenon which directly or indirectly affects the lives of the people in Third World receiving countries.

Tourism cannot be stopped from 'invading' host communities but alternative or more appropriate tourism policies must be developed. This model of alternative tourism evolved by Bina Swadaya is a new concept in development endeavour which needs to be further assimilated, particularly by NGOs in Indonesia. National and international networking should be widely established to support this grassroots campaign in tourism development.

Sustainable tourism is not an illusion or an impossibility if it is carefully planned, implemented, and promoted for the benefit of the local people.

LEGISLATION FOR SUSTAINABLE TOURISM BALEARIC ISLANDS

Eduardo Gamero

Director

EBATUR, Mallorca

in association with Raoul Bianchi

Introduction

Few areas of the world have experienced the development of mass tourism on the scale seen on the coasts of Spain over the past thirty years. Franco's 'Plan Nacional de Estabilization', unveiled in 1959, established a policy of 'crecimiento al cualquier precio' (growth at any price), opening the floodgates on a construction fever that has left the Spanish coastline ravaged by the concrete blight of short-sighted development projects.

The Balearic Islands, in particular Ibiza and Mallorca, have long been the favoured destination of over 5 million (1990) sun-seekers each year, and have some of the worst excesses of the tourist construction boom. One could be forgiven for expressing a certain degree of surprise at their inclusion as a model for 'sustainable tourism'. Particularly relevant is the passage of a series of laws by the Balearic Parliament, in 1991, which imposed substantial new limits on further construction, and which marks a significant turning point in attitudes towards planning and conservation in a region renowned for its flagrant disregard for such concepts.

Rationale

The principal rationale behind the strict legislative constraints on development is to improve the quality of the 'tourist product' which has deteriorated dramatically under the weight of over-construction. The consistent campaigning of a local environmental group, Grupo Ornithologico Balearbeach (GBO), has been decisive in stimulating an environmental consciousness both within the Balearic government and amongst the population as a whole. The latter are becoming increasingly involved in efforts to protect remaining natural areas from developers. The new legislation represents a considerable victory for the environmentalists who have campaigned consistently for the preservation of natural areas, such as Es Trenc, one of the few remaining virgin stretches of beach on Mallorca, and the delicate wetland area of Albufera also on Mallorca. Under the new legislation Es Trenc has been declared a 'natural shoreline' and Albufera, a Natural Park.

Initial indications that change was on its way became apparent during the mid-1980s. Limits were introduced in

1984 requiring new developments to meet a minimum provision to 60 square metres per bed, subsequently increased to 120 square metres per bed the following year. Despite these restrictive measures and the introduction, in 1988, of the controversial Ley de Costas legislation, prohibiting construction within a 100 metre protection zone adjacent to the sea, a group of enterprising Ministers from the Islands' Conservative government decided the only way to ensure the long-term survival of the Balearic's tourism industry would be through the formulation and implementation of tougher legislation independent from the central authorities. So far their endeavours are proving to be relatively successful and, most significantly, the new measures have elevated the issue of environmental protection from the margins of debate to the top of the political agenda.

'Espana Verde'

Although the authorities are beginning to acknowledge the mistakes of the past and have begun to develop an awareness of the need to reconcile commercial interests with environmental concerns, their newly acquired environmental conscience received considerable impetus from primary economic considerations. The loss of competitiveness cited as the main reason for the drop in arrivals from 1988 to 1989, and an appreciating peseta, led to a severe fall in revenue in areas of high tourism concentration such as the Balearic Islands. Although arrivals increased in the following years, the value of investments has declined, providing further evidence of the need for a re-assessment of the industry's priorities. In addition, tourist complaints of inadequate infrastructure, urban and environmental degradation, plus a general decline in the overall standards of service, reached an all time high throughout the country. This prompted Turespana (the Spanish Institute for the Promotion of Tourism) to shift the emphasis of promotion away from the heavily concentrated coasts to the interior. Their slogan 'Espana Verde' is indicative of the changes occurring within the Spanish tourism industry which are aimed at reorganising the overall tourist product.

The Balearics are the only region of Spain to have implemented such progressive legislation. Indeed the other traditionally over-developed regions, particularly the Canaries and the Costa del Sol are looking to the Balearics rather than the central government for advice on how to restructure their ailing resorts and protect remaining natural areas. The measures introduced by the government in the Balearics represents the most far-reaching restrictions to development in the entire country, and illustrates that with resources channelled effectively into the right areas even the most excessively developed areas, such as Magalluf, can be salvaged, and natural areas protected.

Legislation

Under the legislation one third of Mallorca's surface area is now protected from future development. Even land that falls outside the designated 'protected areas' must comply with the 120 square metres per bed restrictions, thus preventing developers from exploiting those areas not encompassed by the new laws. The protective legislation itself is classified into three separate categories according to existing and potential future land uses:

1 **Natural Areas of Special Interest** include those areas deemed to be of outstanding natural value and ecological importance.

2 **Rural Areas of Scenic Interest** include areas of primarily traditional land use activity, but are still deemed of special scenic value.

3 **Areas of Settlement in a Landscape of Interest** include areas of a primarily urban nature although declared of an exceptional scenic value.

Implementation

In these areas no new construction will be permitted except in cases of 'justified need' according to existing land uses, public works and infrastructure requirements. In the heavily concentrated areas of tourist construction millions of pounds (£8m in Magalluf alone) are being spent on urban regeneration projects which include the demarcation of green zones and traffic-free areas. Rigorous inspections have led to the closure of up to 250 hotels (primarily one, two and three star). Others that fail to comply with the new standards will not be granted licences to repaint, but forced to close. This includes those buildings that fall within the 100 metre protection zone prescribed by the Ley de Costas.

In the majority of cases the municipal authorities are responsible for the approval of building licences, granting of permits and infrastructure provision. As a result they are empowered to decide on an alternative use for those hotels that have been forced to close down. Nevertheless, the public administration also recognises that on some occasions infrastructure deficiencies may require resources beyond the scope of these local authorities. In such instances the Balearic Government has proposed to undertake a joint venture with the relevant municipal authority, assuming sixty percent of the cost of each project in accordance with the Special Plan for Investment and Improvements in Tourist Areas.

Although new European Community directives in favour of consumers will increase the pressure for higher standards and tour operator liability, the Balearic legislation is far more comprehensive. Similarly EC directives recommend that a minimum seven per cent of surface area must be protected from further construction, whereas in the Balearics approximately 35 per cent of the surface area is already protected. The Balearics have also received little in the way of financial assistance from the EC for the primary reason that they have one of the highest per capita incomes in Spain from tourism and thus don't qualify for EC development grants.

At a time when other parts of Spain, particularly the Costa del Sol, are still battling against the developers, the Balearic Government has certainly proved far more progressive in attempting to demonstrate that mass tourism can play a more symbiotic role with the environment, natural and man-made. Despite opposition from landowners who felt that they stood to lose the most from building restrictions, the proponents of the legislation held the conviction that if something were not done soon not only would the islands' environment suffer further destruction, but the

long-term survival of an industry that is the life-blood of the islands, would be severely at risk. So far the introduction of legislation has been handled with far more skill than the announcement of the Ley de Costas, which received fierce attacks in the press as well as reports of threats delivered to inspectors.

Controversy

There is still a degree of ongoing controversy and debate within the islands, however, particularly over the creation of the first National Park in the Balearics, Cabrera, and plans to develop more golf courses on Mallorca. Many in the tourist industry feel that it is unfair to limit access entirely to the island, and that tourists are often held disproportionately responsible for damage to the landscape. The government is still considering a petition of 15,000 signatures that has been delivered to them in favour of allowing a limited number of visitors to the island. The issue itself is indicative of the fact that developers are no longer the key players in the decision-making process. The GOB are still locked in opposition to all developments that invade new and untouched natural areas, which has again brought them into direct confrontation with developers proposing 'greener' alternatives to the resorts particularly golf courses. Despite their appearance they still involve a substantial alteration and disturbance of natural habitats.

The new legislation and the changing nature of tourist preferences is shifting the focus, albeit at a steady pace, toward more sustainable forms of tourism in the relatively 'undiscovered' parts of the islands. Old 'fincas' (farmhouses) that have been abandoned as a result of the declining profitability of agriculture, are being restored into rural accommodation, as are other grander buildings in the old towns. The restoration of ancient network of stone footpaths is also opening up interior regions to hikers and walkers more appreciative of the local environment.

Even more adventurous schemes encourage greater involvement of tourists in the preservation of the natural environment, such as EarthWatch, who are encouraging visitors to spend time working and monitoring wildlife in the recently created wetland sanctuary at Albufera.

Conclusion

Many parts of the Balearic Islands remain untouched by tourism and thankfully, under the directives of the new legislation will remain so. Five years ago it was inconceivable that environmental consciousness and restrictive legislation could exist in a region that had all but sold itself to the tourist dollar. The tourist product on offer is now changing in response to environmental concern, although some areas will still continue to cater to the sun, sea and sand market. The authorities feel that the Balearics have the capacity to absorb different types of tourism. Nevertheless capacity will be reduced at the lower end of the market and increased at the luxury end.

Areas where similar legislation urgently needs to be applied are the other over-developed coastal regions and island destinations where tourism is the dominant industry. Above all, such areas must realise, as the Balearics have done, that tourism cannot destroy the environment without ultimately destroying itself, and must therefore learn to co-exist with the scarce resources upon which their very survival depends.

References

1 *Yearbook of Tourism Statistics*, World Tourism Organisation 1991.

2 *The World Travel & Tourism Environment Review*, World Travel and Tourism Council, 1992.

3 International Chamber of Commerce, *Sustainable Development – The Business Approach* (Paris 1989) in Pearce D, Markandya A, Barbier E, *Blueprint for a Green Economy*, Earthscan Publications, 1989, p121.

4 The Natural World, *Portrait of the Planet*, BBC 2, 23rd February, 1992.

5 Jenner P & Smith C, *The Tourism Industry and the Environment*, Economist Intelligence Unit (EIU), Special Report No 2453, 1992, p90.

6 *The Green Light: A guide to sustainable tourism*, Rural Development Commission, English Tourist Board, Countryside Commission, 1991.

7 EIU Report No 2453, 1992, p83.

8 ibid p91.

9 *Tourism and the Environment*, Economist Intelligence Unit, Travel and Tourism Analyst No 5, 1989, p74.

10 Barrett, M, *Aircraft Pollution Report*, World Wide Fund For Nature, 1991.

11 *Roads to Ruin*, World Wide Fund For Nature, 1990.

12 Hoggart S, *Loved to Death*, World, BBC Magazine of Mankind, April 1992, p90.

13 *Managing Tourism and the Environment – A Kenyan Case Study*, EIU Travel and Tourism Analyst No 2 1991.

14 Pleumaron A, *Tourism, Resorts and the Worldwide Golf Mania*, discussion paper presented at the People's Forum Third World Tourism Workshop, Bangkok, 17th October, 1991, p10.

15 ibid p11.

16 ibid p11.

17 Rajendra C, *Tourism and Human Rights*, paper presented at ITB Berlin, March 1992.

18 Patterson, Rev K, *Aloha for Sale*, In Focus, No 4, 1992.

19 EIU Report No 2453, 1992, p96.

20 The Natural World, *Portrait of the Planet*, BBC 2, 23rd February 1992.

21 Arndell, R, *Tourism as a Development Concept in the South Pacific*, The Courier No 122, 1990, pp 83-86.

22 Forrest J, Communication to Tourism Concern, 1992.

23 The Natural World, *Portrait of the Planet*, BBC 2, 23rd February, 1992.

24 Pearce D, Markandya A, Barbier E, *Blueprint for a Green Economy*, Earthscan Publications, 1989, p75.

25 EIU Report No 2453, 1992, p122.

26 ibid p128.

27 *Antarctica, The Last Place on Earth*, The Guardian, 28th January, 1992.

28 EIU Report No 2453, 1992, p109.

29 ibid p42.

30 ibid p91.

31 Jones A, *Alternative Approaches to Tourism Development with Reference to Wales*, in *Problems of Tourism*, Vol 12, Institute of Tourism, Warsaw, 1990.

32 EIU Report No 2453, 1992, p122.

33 Council Directive of 27th June 1985 (85/337/40), Official Journal of the European Communities, No L 175/40.

34 EIU Report No 2453, 1992, p76.

35 *Ecotourism in Belize*, Horizon, BBC 2, 11th March 1991.

36 Ruitenbeek H J, *Economic Analysis of Tropical Conservation Initiatives: Examples from West Africa*, WWF UK (World Wide Fund For Nature), Godalming, UK 1990.

37 Ekins P, *Wealth Beyond Measure, An Atlas of New Economics*, Gaia Books 1992, p37.

38 Barrett F, *A Balancing Act in Cyprus*, The Independent, 19th May, 1990.

39 Erlichman J, *More People will leave the Land*, The Guardian, 21st May, 1992.

40 Lean, G, Ghazi, P, *Fallow Future for British Farmland*, The Observer, 24th May, 1992.

41 Arndell, R, *Tourism as a Development Concept in the South Pacific*, The Courier No 122, 1990, pp 83-86.

42 Dunning J H & McQueen M, *Transnational Corporations in International Tourism*, United Nations Centre on Transnational Corporations, 1982.

43 *The economic realities of food for tourism in the Bahamas*, The Food Programme, BBC Radio 4, 19th June, 1992.

44 Ekins P, op cit, p125.

45 Jones A, *Alternative Approaches to Tourism Development with Reference to Wales*, in *Problems of Tourism*, Vol 12, Institute of Tourism, Warsaw, 1990.

46 EIU Report, No 2453, 1992, p73.

47 Pleumaron A, *Filipinos Organise for Solidarity Tourism*, Contours (ECTWT) Vol 5 No 5/6, 1992.

48 Olerokonga T, *What About the Massai?*, In Focus, No 4, 1992.

49 Patterson Rev K, *Aloha for Sale*, In Focus, No 4, 1992.

50 Parnwell, M, Communication to Tourism Concern, 1992.

51 Shoup J, in O'Grady A, *The Challenge of Tourism*, Ecumenical Coalition on Third World Tourism (ECTWT) 1990, p18.

52 *Sustainable Tourism Newsletter*, Eco-Institute of Costa Rica, May 1992

53 *Environmental Policy in the European Community*, DG Information, Communication, Culture Publications Division, March 1990, p33.

54 Eckstein M, Communication to Tourism Concern, 1992.

55 *Tourism and Developing Countries*, EIU Travel and Tourism Analyst No 6, 1989, p77.

56 Sinclair M Thea, *Tourism Development in Kenya*, World Bank, Washington, 1990.

57 EIU op cit, p77.

58 Robson J, Communication to Tourism Concern, 1992.

59 Council Directive of 13th June 1990 (990/314/EEC), Official Journal of the European Communities, No L 158/59, 23rd June 1990.

60 Patterson, Rev K, Tourism's *Negative Impact on Native Hawaiians*, paper presented to ITB, Berlin, 11th March, 1992.

61 Somerville H, Communication to Tourism Concern, 1992.

62 Towner J and France L, *Rapid Rural Appraisal Techniques: Their Approach to Geographical Studies of Tourism*, in Tourism Recreation Research, Vol 17, No 1, Lucknow, India, 1992.

63 Hills A, *The new truth about the lie of the land*, The Guardian, 30th July 1992.

IN FOCUS is published by Tourism Concern.

Bibliography

ACE Group/WWF UK, *Thinking Globally, Enabling Locally: Improving support for local environmental action*, WWF UK, 1992.

Britain and the Brundtland Report, A Programme of Action for Sustainable Development, Volume 1, International Institute for Environment and Development, London.

World Commission on Environment and Development, *Our Common Future (The Brundtland Report)*, 1987.

Cater E, *Sustainable Tourism in the Third World: Problems and Prospects*, Dept of Geography, University of Reading, 1991.

Ekins P, *Wealth Beyond Measure, An Atlas of New Economics*, Gaia Books Ltd, 1992.

Jackson B, *Poverty and the Planet, A Question of Survival*, World Development Movement, Penguin Books, 1990.

Jenner P and Smith C, *The Tourism Industry and The Environment*, Economist Intelligence Unit, Specialist Report No 2453, 1992.

O'Grady A, (ed), *The Challenge of Tourism, Learning Resources for Study and Action*, Ecumenical Coalition on Third World Tourism, Bangkok, 1990.

Pearce D, Barbier E and Markandya A, *Sustainable Development, Economics and Environment in the Third World*, Earthscan Publications, 1990.

Pearce D, Markandya A and Barbier E, *Blueprint for a Green Economy*, Earthscan Publications, 1989.

Further reading

Archibald J, *Proceedings of the Second Annual Tourism Management Colloquium: Corporate Responsibility, Tourism Product Development and the Environment, Montreal, Quebec, 25th May 1988*, Montreal, Quebec, Canada: McGill University, Management Graduate Department, 1989.

Beller W, D'Ayala P, Hein P, (editors) *Sustainable Development and Environmental Management of Small Islands*, Carnforth, Lancashire, UK: Parthenon Publishing Group; Paris, France: UNESCO, 1990.

Boo E, *Ecotourism: The Potentials and Pitfalls*, 2 volumes, Baltimore, MD, USA: WWF-US, 1990.

Chambers R, *Short-cut and participatory methods of gaining social information for projects* in Cernea M M, (ed) *Sociological variables in rural development*, 2nd ed, World Bank, 1991.

De Kadt E, *Making the Alternative Sustainable: Lessons from Development for Tourism*, Institute of Development Studies, 1990.

Dwyer L, Forsyth P, *Effectiveness of Environmental Policy Instruments – A Case Study of Australian Tourism*, Discussions Paper Series, School of Business & Technology, University of Western Sydney, Macarther, Cambelltown, NSW, Australia, 1990.

Fisher J F, *Sherpas: Reflections on Change in Himalayan Nepal*, Berkley, California, USA: University of California Press, 1990.

Harrison D, (ed) *Tourism & The Less Developed Countries*, Belhaven Press, London, UK, 1992.

Sidaway R, *Good Conservation Practice for Sport and Recreation*, London, UK, 1990.